WILDERNESS MISSION

*"This house is a resort for the whole country,
where Christians find a hospital in their sickness,
a refuge in the height of alarms, and a hospice
when they come to visit us."*

Rev. Paul Ragueneau, S.J., Superior
of the Huron Mission, Sainte-Marie.
Written April 16, 1648 for the Jesuit
Relations of 1647-48.

WILDERNESS MISSION

THE STORY
OF SAINTE-MARIE-AMONG-
THE-HURONS

JOHN F. HAYES

THE RYERSON PRESS
TORONTO / WINNIPEG / VANCOUVER

© THE RYERSON PRESS, 1969

SBN 7700 3166 8

ACKNOWLEDGMENTS

The author and the publisher wish to acknowledge the help of
John R. Sloan, Director of Huronia Historical Parks, and Basil
Mason, Public Relations officer of that body; they were both
of tremendous assistance in providing material for this book.
The publisher wishes to record his gratitude to Vernon Mould
and William Cranston for their assistance in the initiating of
this book.

   Illustrations were obtained with permission from the Ontario
Department of Tourism and Information, except for the following:
Royal Ontario Museum for pages 16 and 18; Toronto
Public Library for 2, 11 and 23: Oxford University Press (Canadian
Branch) for the map on page 33 from *Saint-Marie Among the Hurons*
by Wilfrid Jury and Elsie McLeod Jury.

   "The Huron Carol", words translated and arranged by J.E. Middleton,
is used by permission of the copyright owner,
Frederick Harris Music Co. Limited, Oakville.

Printed and bound in Canada by
The Ryerson Press, Toronto

PREFACE

If the European-style community of Sainte-Marie had risen within easy reach of Quebec, in the middle 1600's, it would have been a highlight of early Canadian enterprise. But it was built more than 800 miles away in the deep wilderness, where it could be reached only by canoe. This makes the existence of Sainte-Marie little short of miraculous.

No other mission in Canada can match Sainte-Marie in historical significance. Its short ten-year life, which ended in flames, is a story of devotion, courage and purpose that will live forever among Canada's most outstanding achievements.

Here in the years 1639 to 1649, artisans from Normandy built as they had built in France, erecting simple but beautiful, high-gabled buildings similar to those of their native land; here an unknown engineer built what is believed to have been the first locked waterway in North America; here were established the first hospital and pharmacy in Canada's hinterland; and here was North America's first religious shrine.

Sainte-Marie has risen again in our time, and its reconstruction is a tribute to the men who painstakingly searched for its secrets, and then rebuilt it, stone by stone and timber by timber.

To view Sainte-Marie today as more than a casual tourist and to imagine life there as it once was, one must know something of its beginnings. It is a sacred spot, for this ground was once walked upon by Brébeuf, Lalemant, Daniel, Garnier and Chabanel— those devout Jesuit priests who met torture and death at the hands of the Iroquois.

The story of the Jesuits and of Sainte-Marie-Among-the-Hurons is also the story of the Huron Indians and of their land, Huronia. This once-prosperous and once-numerous tribe was the sole reason for the Jesuit mission, and the history of the two groups is intricately and fatefully interwoven.

J.F.H.

TORONTO
SEPTEMBER, 1969

CONTENTS

Hurons in aboriginal dress.

PART ONE

HURONIA—
THE
ANCIENT
OUENDAKE

Before 1600, the 30,000 Indians who lived in that part of Ontario now referred to as Huronia were known as Ouendats, an ancient name that means "Dwellers on a Peninsula". They called their land Ouendake. They were descendants of the Iroquois who had crossed the Detroit River centuries earlier to settle in the northwest area of southern Ontario.

One old tale tells how they came to be called Hurons. A French seaman, when he first saw a band of Ouendats at Tadoussac in 1600, was highly amused by the way in which the Indians dressed their hair; it stood up in stiff ridges, like the bristles on the neck of a wild boar. "Quelles hures!" he exclaimed, "What boar-heads!" But it is more likely that the name came from the French word *huron*, which was used as early as 1358 to describe bristly, unkempt and troublesome peasants. In any event, the Ouendats became known as Hurons, and their land was called Huronia.

The country of the Hurons lay generally south of Georgian Bay. Along the eastern frontier were Lake Simcoe and Lake Couchiching. The northern border was defined by the Severn River, and the shores of Matchedash Bay and Nottawasaga Bay, to the present site of Collingwood. The border then ran south to the highlands, then east to what is now Barrie, Ontario.

To the west of Huronia lived some 20,000 Petuns or Tobacco Indians. Farther south, between the Detroit and Niagara Peninsulas, was the land of the Neutrals, so called because they took no part in Indian wars. All three tribes—Huron, Petun and Neutral—were related and shared the same customs and language. The Iroquois, who lived south of Lake Ontario and the St. Lawrence River, and to whom they were related, were their common enemy, and fierce battles were fought frequently between the rival tribes.

When Champlain visited the Hurons in 1615, he found that they occupied eighteen villages, all within a few miles of one another. Eight were fortified with palisades and ramparts, and to these would come the inhabitants of the other villages in times of danger. The settlements were located on high ground close to a good stream with a spring of clear water nearby. At intervals of ten to thirty years, when the inhabitants found themselves too far away from wood, or when the land was exhausted and corn would no longer grow in the unfertilized soil, the towns were moved to new territory.

The wooden-palisaded villages were usually circular or oval in shape, with walls as high as thirty-five feet. The palisades were of triple thickness. One line of posts was set upright in a trench and a second row was placed three or four feet away and leaned towards the perpendicular wall. The poles were then lashed together at the top. This was repeated on the other side so that the poles were interlaced. The wall was reinforced by large, thick pieces of bark to a height of about nine feet. The trunks of heavy trees were laid in the spaces between the three lines of poles, and platforms or galleries were built on the inside. From these platforms, stones could be thrown in time of siege, and water could be poured on the walls if they were set on fire by the attackers. For entry there was only one small gate, which could be quickly barred up.

Each village contained from twenty to thirty dwellings set irregularly apart to avoid complete destruction in case of fire. These lodges, or longhouses, varied in length from 150 to 180 feet and were twenty feet wide. They were constructed of saplings placed butt-end into holes which had been dug three feet apart and in two parallel rows. The tops of the saplings were pulled together and bound with vines to form a rounded roof. Horizontal poles were then lashed to the uprights to strengthen the framework. The framework was covered with sheets of overlapping bark, and openings were left in the roof to allow smoke to escape.

Inside, a raised platform of thick sheets of bark ran the length of the lodge on both sides. In summer, the Indians slept on the

The skeleton of a Huron longho
showing authentic construction de

platforms but in winter they huddled on mats close to the cooking fires in the centre. As many as eight to twenty-four families, or between fifty to 150 people crowded around the fires, two families sharing one fire. Under the space made by the sleeping platform, dry wood was stored for the winter. At each end of the lodge stood large bark casks for keeping corn and smoked fish. Corncobs, dried herbs, fish, meat, roots, skins and clothing hung from the rafters out of the way of mice.

There was absolutely no privacy in a Huron lodge, with men, women, children and dogs crowded around the fires. In winter it was smoke-filled and draughty, crawling with vermin, and dirty from the continuous soot produced by the numerous fires.

The Hurons were mainly peaceful farmers and fishermen, depending largely on agriculture for their existence. The cornfields around their villages often stretched for two or more miles in every direction. Fields were divided among the families, each sowing and reaping according to its needs. The chief crop was corn, which assured an adequate supply of food at all times. Squash, beans, sunflowers and tobacco were also grown. Surplus stock was traded with neighbouring tribes.

Corn could be prepared in many different ways. Usually it was pounded, mixed with fish, meat, fresh or sun-dried wild fruits, and served as a soupy porridge called sagamite. Leindohy was a delicacy made from corn soaked and fermented in mud. Other foods such as wild pumpkins, blackberries, blueberries, raspberries, water-lily roots, edible moss and acorns also were popular among Huron cooks.

In the fall, when Georgian Bay teemed with whitefish, there were fishing expeditions. The fishnets were woven from wild nettles, which had been pounded, shredded, and rolled into threads. These nets, sometimes as long as 1,200 feet, were a valuable trade item. In winter, fish were caught through holes in the ice, by fish hooks and harpoons fashioned from bone.

Unlike the nomadic tribes in the north, who depended for their food on what they hunted, the Hurons were completely self-sufficient, because of their vast cornfields. Game was relatively scarce in this region, but whenever possible the food supply was supplemented by hunting. Deer hunts were organized in which the animals were driven into pounds in the woods and slaughtered. Young bears were trapped, kept in captivity and fattened. Beavers were caught for food, and their pelts used for trade. Dogs were considered a delicacy, and were bred for food by the thousands.

The Hurons ate sparingly, usually twice a day, but often indulged in gluttonous feasts when game was plentiful. Bowls and plates were made of bark; spoons were fashioned from bone and wood. Food was cooked in fragile clay pots. As these could not be placed directly over a fire, red-hot stones were used as the cooking medium; they were dropped into the pot's contents, fished out again as they cooled, and replaced by more red-hot stones. Indeed, where Huron "fire-stones" are found today, nearly always an ancient Huron settlement is discovered. In addition to using stones, the Hurons baked their food in mud and roasted it on spits. When meat was either baked or roasted, the bones were often cracked to obtain the hot marrow.

Modern civilization is based on, and in fact depends on, agriculture. Thus it is significant to notice that the Hurons, also dependent on the soil, practised a form of food storing, similar in principle to modern storage facilities. They made caches of corn, beans and nut kernels in bark-lined pits, and also dried fruits and berries. Often these pits were under the floors of their lodges. They excelled in the art of smoking meats over smouldering fires, in sun-drying wild berries on bark trays and in sun-drying meats on racks ten feet high.

Physically the Hurons were a strong, well-proportioned people. Their skin was the colour of bronze. They used oil and grease to anoint their bodies, and when on the war-path painted their faces in vivid colours. The men paid a great deal of attention to their hair, wearing it in two rolls above their ears, with a close-cropped ridge down the centre. Wampum necklaces and ornaments were favourites with the women, who wore their hair in one thick braid hanging down their backs.

The native tribes of Eastern Canada.

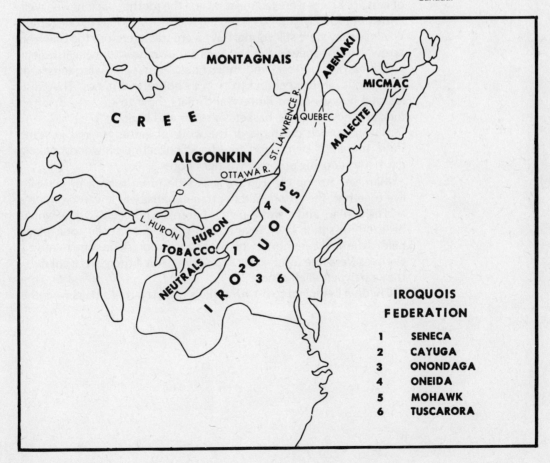

In summer they wore little clothing, but in spring and autumn they dressed in light garments made from tanned skins. In winter, they wore fur cloaks woven in strips of rabbit fur. Furs were sewn by lacing strips of hide through holes punched in the skins by bone awls. Garments were often fringed and painted with designs. Pins were made from straightened fish bones. Bands of porcupine quills, dyed a bright scarlet, were a highly valued decoration, and were often transferred from one robe to another for different occasions.

The basic Huron garment was a single beaver skin, worn over the shoulders as a mantle, and breeches made of deer skin. The robe was almost shapeless, and had detachable sleeves. The women dressed like the men with the added decoration of wampum beads, made from bits of polished shells. Some necklaces contained thousands of pieces of shell. Tattooing was not common among the Hurons, although a few practised it.

Huron family life followed well-defined customs. Families were usually small, and a man could take only one wife. Children grew up in a very free society, and they were never punished. Indeed, this lack of discipline extended throughout Huron society; no one had to obey the laws, except as he chose, and no individual punishment was meted out for crimes. There was no organization set up to enforce the law, but the whole community was required to atone for the misdeeds of any of its people—usually by giving presents to those who had suffered. A deep affection existed in Huron families. Mothers carried their babies on highly decorated cradle-boards, with the child carefully oiled and packed in moss, and the soft down of cattails. Babies were fed meat, which the mother had chewed well, and corn broth, which was often fed mouth-to-mouth by the father.

While they were still young, boys were trained to use the bow and arrow, and the spear. Later they were shown how to make fish-nets, warclubs, bows, arrows and snowshoes. Young girls were taught to pound corn into meal and to help in household duties. They also learned how to make pottery and mats, how to dress and soften furs, and how to make baskets of reeds and bark.

Huron women did most of the work of gathering and grinding corn, preparing hemp and tree bark, collecting firewood, making garments, cooking and many other chores.

Marriage among the Hurons was little more than a promise to live together. The groom had to prove his ability as a warrior, hunter and fisherman, and it was the girl's parents who decided if he would be a fitting son-in-law! Several trial marriages usually took place before the final ceremony, which was a feast for friends and relatives. Couples were free to separate at any time, but if there were children, they rarely left each other.

Children belonged to their mother's clan; a father's heirs were the children of his sisters, not his own. This rather complicated system of inheritance resulted in a wide-spread kinship, or clan, in which the women were far more important than the men.

Before the coming of white men, the Hurons were a stone-age people who used stone, bone, wood, clay and other natural materials to make everything needed. Their ingenuity and methods of craftsmanship stemmed from centuries of experience and invention.

Stone, the major material, was used in making axes, adzes, hammers, smoking pipes and other heavier items. Flint, secured by trade, was used to make knives, scrapers, arrow-heads and small, sharp drills. Coloured stones were fashioned into beads, ground, polished and strung on lengths of skin.

Bone was also used with great skill. Awls, needles, harpoons, fish-hooks and bodkins for making fishnets were some of the Hurons' bone instruments. Chisels were made from beaver teeth; and hoes, from the shoulder blades of deer. Jewellery, bracelets, pendants, combs and beads were made from the bones of fowl and from shells. Antler tips were fashioned as punches, scrapers and other cutting tools.

But it was wood that formed the backbone of Huron industry. From it the Hurons made their homes, canoes, bows and arrows, toboggans, snowshoes, spear-handles, clubs and tools, paddles, bowls, pounders, mortars and a dozen other necessities. Rope was made from tamarack roots, wild grape vines and the inner bark of elm, basswood and cedar—the latter being used widely in weaving mats for floors, beds and doorways. Corn husk fibres were woven into material.

From clay mixed with stone fragments, the Hurons fashioned pottery and decorated it with shells. Some evidence of cold-pounded copper tools and ornaments have been discovered in Huronia, probably secured from present-day northern Michigan.

In their daily life, the Hurons liked games and were inveterate gamblers, often staking everything they owned in games of chance. They invented lacrosse and played tribe against tribe with as many as 200 men taking part at one time. Goals were as far as a mile-and-a-half apart, and games sometimes lasted for several days. Play was very rough and serious injuries—and even fatalities—resulted.

Modern ice hockey came from a game which young Hurons played using a curved wooden stick and a wooden ball on hard-packed winter snow or ice. Snow snake was another popular Huron game: long, slender sticks were flung down a trough in the snow, the winner of the game being the one whose stick went the greatest distance.

Another favourite was the bowl game in which five or six fruit stones were tossed from a bowl. Each stone, slightly flattened, was painted black on one side and a lighter colour on the other. When all the stones came up one colour, the man who had tossed was the winner. The medicine-men of the Hurons believed there were great healing powers in the games of lacrosse and bowls. Often matches were played to aid those who were ill, to influence the weather or to pay respect to certain individuals.

The Hurons' religion was a mixture of superstition and witchcraft. The people believed that spirits, or *Oki,* dwelt in the forest, in rivers and in animals and fish; the favour of such spirits could be gained by gifts or sacrifices. Spirits were everywhere, controlling man's every act. Feasts to honour various spirits were frequent. The Hurons constantly carried charms or amulets in a pouch; these certain charms—stones, the beak of a raven, the skin of a snake—were believed to ensure success in hunting, fishing, trading and other activities.

The Hurons believed in the existence of a Great Spirit, the Creator of all things, which they referred to as *Orenda.* But more important to them were the spirits that lived in the rivers, trees, hills and stones, to which they made sacrifices and gave gifts.

Dancing was an important part of the Huron religion. A wide variety of dances was performed to appease the spirits, to improve hunting and fishing, to ensure success in war, to celebrate a wedding or a birth and to cure the sick. The steps in the dances were precise, and extreme care was taken to do them properly, lest the spirit to whom they were directed be offended. Dances were the property of certain families, who performed them under the guidance of a Dancing Master. Some dances were remarkable, such as the "Dance of Fire", in which the participants carried live coals in their mouths and plunged their arms into boiling water.

Dreams, too, were part of the Hurons' religion; they were considered as directives and prophecies. Every dream had to be obeyed blindly, no matter what might be involved. Warriors returned home from raids and hunts were abandoned, if dreams foretold misfortune or an empty bag. Feasts, dances and games were held when dreams suggested such activities.

At the centre of the religious life were the powerful medicine-men and their secret societies. Admission to a medicine society was allowed only after a young man had experienced and described certain vivid dreams. Illness sometimes proved a youth's eligibility. Often a sick or wounded youth, delirious and babbling with fever, would be hailed as one whose body had been used by the spirits to talk to the medicine-men. If he recovered, he would be admitted to one of the medicine societies with great ceremony.

The medicine-men were divided into three classes: those charged with creating rain or sunshine; seers whose responsibility it was to find lost objects and divine the future; and practitioners who were

10

supposed to diagnose disease, remove the cause and cure the patient. While incantations, rattle shaking, blowing ashes in the face, and other such practices were the stock-in-trade of the medicine-men, they did not depend on these alone. They were skilled in preparing herbs and roots for internal medicine, and in addition performed some remarkable operations. They built primitive but effective steam baths, and used this therapy both as a preventative and a cure. They isolated people with infectious diseases; and they were highly skilled in treating infections and wounds with incisions, and in applying herb poultices.

The death of a Huron was a time for feast and ritual. The body was wrapped in fur, held for three days of mourning and lamentation, then placed in a bark box mounted on four posts. Food, arrow-heads, beads, pottery and other items were left for the spirits to use. Sometimes burial in the earth was carried out, but not often.

The most impressive of all Huron religious ceremonies was the great "Feast of the Dead", which was held every ten or twelve years. At a chosen spot a deep pit was dug and lined with the finest fur robes. Bodies were taken from all the village cemeteries, what flesh remained was scraped off the skeleton, and the bodies were rewrapped in furs and reverently carried to the common burial pit. After a period of feasting and dancing, the bones of the dead were placed in the pit. Presents were distributed to the relatives of the dead, but the choicest were given to the chiefs who had organized the event. Hurons believed that the dead eventually reached the Village of Souls, a place similar to earthly villages, where they spent their time hunting and fishing.

Long before the white man came to Huronia, trading had been the mainstay of the Huron economy. It was the natural outgrowth of a life based on agriculture, for corn provided a light, compact, nourishing food which could be carried on long canoe trips without going bad. The settled village life allowed the Hurons to grow crops, and to harvest and store them. Surplus corn, fishnets, shell beads and other products were exchanged for furs from the Nipissings and Algonkians. The Hurons became the middlemen in trade with the Petuns and Neutrals and jealously guarded their monopoly, ruling that these two nations must not deal directly with the northern tribes.

Trade was highly organized, with families allotted certain trade routes. General plans were made at tribal council meetings, and strict control was exercised over all trading activities. Distance never deterred the Hurons and they organized trips hundreds of miles west to Sault Ste. Marie, to the upper part of Lake Michigan and to the Saguenay River. Before the French arrived on the St. Lawrence, Hurons had exchanged goods with tribes who lived in the foothills of the Rocky Mountains, with the Indians of the Atlantic seaboard, with tribes living on the fringes of the Arctic and with others far to the south.

In summer, the Hurons travelled in birch-bark canoes. These were eight to nine paces long, and a pace-and-a-half wide in the middle. While light enough to carry around portages, they were quite sturdy and easy to repair on the journey. In winter the Hurons wore snow-shoes and pulled sleds and toboggans over the ice and snow.

Primitive though it may seem to us, the Hurons possessed a reasonably effective form of government. The tribe was divided into four clans: the Bear, which was the largest, the Rock, the Cord and the Deer. A fifth group called the One White Lodge clan was comprised of Indians from the other four. Each territory had its own great chief, with lesser chiefs governing the villages. Important matters were settled in either tribal or village council meetings held in large village longhouses set aside for such purposes. When great secrecy was required, such meetings were held deep in the forest. The Hurons were eloquent debaters, showing good judgment and moderation, and paying great respect to the counsel of elders.

Chiefs and lesser chiefs had their own duties. To some fell the care of village matters—organizing feasts, dances, entertainment, sports and the burial of the dead. Others, designated as war chiefs, handled military matters—defending the villages, recruiting young braves for war parties, planning attacks on marauding Iroquois and making treaties.

Although there was no machinery set up to enforce the laws, Huron rules of behaviour were generally followed to the letter. Theft and murder demanded retribution rather than individual punishment. If a thief were caught, he might lose all his possessions if his victim wanted to claim them! In the case of a murder, the whole district had to appease the victim's family or village by wholesale gift-giving. All-in-all, a considerable measure of law and order prevailed.

A more or less continuous war was waged between the Hurons and the Iroquois. Every summer 500 to 600 young Hurons infiltrated Iroquois territory, where they broke up into parties of six or seven, and waylaid men, women and children on the trails—either killing them or carrying them back to Huronia for torture and death. The Iroquois harassed the Hurons in the same manner.

This sort of skirmishing brought excitement to their lives, but on the whole, the Hurons were a peaceful tribe. They were intelligent—as shown in their skilful use of the materials at hand for food, clothing and shelter. They were self-sufficient and built their economy mainly on farming, fishing and trading.

*Saint-Marie lay beside the Wye River, with
Mud Lake and marshland beyond.*

PART TWO

THE CHANGING WILDERNESS

First Changes For centuries Huron life remained unchanged. Then, about 1600, news reached Huronia that strange men with pale faces were setting up trading-posts on the St. Lawrence River, and that they had miraculous tools, cloth and ornaments to exchange for furs. The Hurons lost no time in paddling to Tadoussac on the Saguenay River where a handful of French Huguenot traders had established a post. They were quick to realize that the white men offered greater treasures than the Indians of other tribes. Slowly the stone-age life of Huronia began to change; the fur brigades returned from Tadoussac carrying shining knives, copper kettles, needles, trinkets, beads, wonderful dazzling mirrors and cloth of scarlet and gold. It was not until much later that the coveted firearms were entrusted to the Christianized Hurons.

The full weight of Huron trading began to swing towards the St. Lawrence. It followed a route from Georgian Bay, up the French River to Lake Nipissing, then by smaller streams to the Ottawa River and down this waterway to the St. Lawrence. As Huron voyageurs passed through Algonkian country they paid toll to

The defeat of the Iroquois at Lake Champlain. From Champlain's Les Voyages, *Paris, 1613.*

ensure safe passage. Great fur brigades soon plied between Huronia and the French posts, carrying pelts of beaver, buffalo and seal to the whites in return for European goods. Since the Hurons were already established as middleman in trade, they became even more jealous of their position, never allowing the French to deal directly with the tribes to the north and west.

By the time Champlain arrived in 1608 to found Quebec, a well-organized and lucrative fur trade with the Hurons was firmly established. But in order to establish a settlement and spread the white man's religion, Champlain had to encourage the tribe's friendship still further. In this case, it was inevitable that he found himself siding with the Hurons against the Iroquois. In the summer of 1608, with the "Habitation" at Quebec barely erected, he joined a Huron attack on the Iroquois in what is now New York State. His firearms won the battle.

The French gunshots intensified the ancient hostility between Huron and Iroquois. Who could foresee the terrible tragedies that lay ahead, their causes already deeply imbedded in the very foundations of the country's economy? The Indians quickly became dependent on, even addicted to, the white man's tools. The pressure to catch the furs which bought those tools grew. The white man's arrival heightened Indian jealousies, and small skirmishes grew to all-out tribal warfare hitherto unknown to the Indians. It became a battle of white against white, Indian against Indian, white plus Indian against white plus Indian, all centred around the furs. What would happen when the furs grew scarce? Where and how would it end?

On the morning of June 30, 1608, a scarred, weather-beaten little sailing ship, low in the water with a heavy cargo of supplies, eased away from Tadoussac at the mouth of the Saguenay River, crossed the bay where white whales basked in the sunshine and headed up the broad St. Lawrence. The vessel was commanded by Samuel de Champlain, and with him were thirty carpenters, stonemasons and artisans. Three days later, the ship rounded a high promontory, swung shoreward and dropped anchor off a tree-covered strand which lay between the river and the towering cape behind.

Longboats splashed into the water; unloading started almost before the anchor had settled. Laden to the gunwales, the boats moved between the ship and shore. Supplies of food and tools began to pile up beneath the chestnut trees. By the following afternoon the ship was empty and on her way back to Tadoussac for another load. On shore, Champlain's axemen worked, felling the great trees and adzing the trunks into squared timbers. Another group was digging a cellar for the storehouse, while Champlain hurried about the site with plans of his "Habitation" in his hands.

So began Quebec, and so began Canada as well, for from this first French settlement on the St. Lawrence River came the first explorations of the vast, unknown wilderness to the west and north.

For seven years after its founding, Quebec was without priests. The forty inmates of the "Habitation" were Protestant Huguenots who wanted no interference with their trade with the Indians, and they resisted all Champlain's efforts to bring spiritual guidance to the settlement. From his earliest days in Canada, Champlain's ardent desire was to convert the tribes around him to Christianity. He often proclaimed, "The salvation of one soul is of more value than the conquest of an empire." He saw the individual in this light:

They were living without faith or law, without God, without religion, like brute beasts. So I came to the conclusion that I would be doing very wrong if I did not work to find some means to bring them to the knowledge of God.

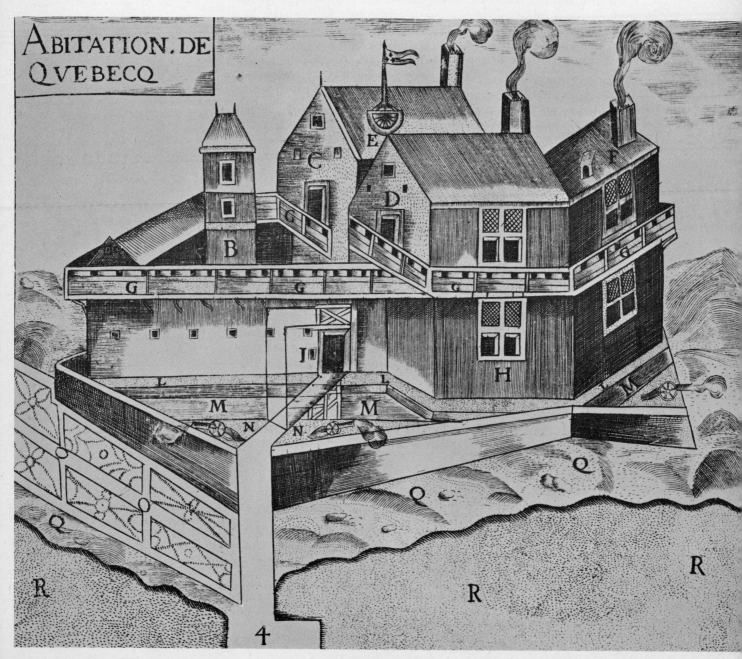

The "Habitation" at Quebec. From
Champlain's Les Voyages, Paris, 1963.

The Récollets   Champlain found the answer to his problem while in France in 1614. The Récollet frères in his home town of Brouage were eager to carry their message of Christ into the wilds. Champlain managed to raise sufficient money for food and equipment to support four missionaries. On May 25, 1615, the Récollets arrived in Quebec: Fathers Denis Jamet, Jean d'Obleau, Joseph le Caron and Brother Pacifique du Plessis.

Five years before the Récollets' arrival, Etienne Brûlé, a young man who had been with the original group at Quebec, had received Champlain's permission to live with the Indians and learn their language. Brûlé was entrusted to the care of the Algonkian chieftain, Iroquet, and lived among the Indians for a year. He returned in June, 1611, and during the following four years roamed the wilderness, spending part of this time in Huronia. He returned to Quebec in 1615 and told Champlain about the Hurons' highly organized fur trade, and of their role as middlemen for all the tribes for hundreds of miles around.

Indeed, Champlain was already aware of the Huron's importance in the growing trade of the Company of Rouen and St. Malo, which ran New France at the time. He was also aware that the Hurons were the most promising people to convert. They were the "solid burghers" among the Indians, compared with the more nomadic and backward Crees. Huronia was composed of permanent settlements and was the natural centre of the fur trade. This area would provide the most fertile ground for a mission, for once the Hurons were converted, the missionaries could fan out to all the distant territories reached by the Huron trader. It was this combination of circumstances which led Champlain to recommend that Huronia be the site of the first inland mission.

The Récollets agreed. It was decided that one of the frères would begin his mission back at Tadoussac, two would remain in Quebec and the fourth, Joseph le Caron, would go to Huronia. He was so eager to begin his mission that he could not be restrained even by Champlain, who advised him to remain for a short time in Quebec to become acclimatized and toughened. On July 6 he set out for the land of the Hurons with a returning fur brigade.

After weeks of arduous travel, le Caron and his native escorts reached the triple-palisaded town of Carhagouha, a few miles inland from Nottawasaga Bay. He was warmly welcomed by the Indians, who built him a large cabin apart from the village, and here he began the first mission in Huronia.

Champlain decided to explore the area himself. He set out from Quebec only a few days after le Caron, and arrived at Carhagouha early in August. On August 12, 1615, the first Mass ever to be held in present-day Ontario was celebrated in le Caron's crude lodge, with Champlain and his party in attendance.

Within about three weeks, Champlain joined a Huron war party bent on an invasion of Iroquois country south of Lake Ontario, but the attack was defeated and the invaders routed. Champlain was severely wounded and had to be carried for several days on the long retreat. When he finally reached Huronia, he found that the Hurons wanted him to winter among them. He agreed and took up his abode at the village of Cahiague, near what is now Orillia.

Early in January he went to live with le Caron at Carhagouha and from there visited several villages of the Tobacco Nation, observing the land, customs and life of the tribe. Finally, on May 22, 1616, he and le Caron set out for Quebec.

Le Caron had had little time to influence the Hurons, but the thin thread of Christian communication had been laid. In Quebec, the Huguenot traders were highly hostile to the spread of the Roman Catholic religion. They placed insurmountable obstacles in the way of the struggling Récollets. Champlain battled with authorities in France, but he was helpless; and the fur-traders, who provided work for almost everyone in Quebec, saw to it that the self-sacrificing Récollets got no help from anyone. Supplies were denied them; no Indian dared take them west again, and they had few funds. It was out of the question to attempt to return to Huronia. So the frères bravely worked on with roving bands of Micmac, Abnaki and Nipissing Indians closer to home, but made little headway in converting them.

For seven harsh years, the grey-robed frères struggled on, before help finally came from France. In 1623, Father Nicolas Viel and Brother Gabriel Sagard arrived in New France, funds were at hand, and the way to Huronia was clear once more. Le Caron re-established his mission at Carhagouha; Viel went to the village of Toanché; Sagard began his work in the settlement of Ossossané. The results were most disheartening. The priests soon realized that the task was too great for three men with no support and limited funds.

In June of 1624, the year after their arrival in Huronia, le Caron and Sagard reluctantly joined the annual Huron fur-fleet leaving for Quebec. Viel chose to stay behind in his little mission at Toanché and wait for help.

On reaching Quebec, le Caron and Sagard met the other Récollets in the little convent on the St. Charles River. They decided to appeal for help to the greatest of all missionary orders, the powerful Society of Jesus. While Viel, alone in a squalid Huron lodge held intact a slender thread of faith, his companion Sagard travelled to France to urge his superiors to send Jesuit help.

The Jesuits agreed to come to Canada and take up the mission. **The Black** Alarmed at this turn of events, the Huguenot traders of Quebec, **Robes** through their friends in France, set out to stop the plan. They had successfully crippled the efforts of the gentle Récollets, but to discourage the aggressive and powerful Jesuit Fathers would be quite another matter.

Pressure began at once. The captain of the Huguenot vessel on which the Jesuit Fathers had arranged passage refused to allow them to come aboard. The Viceroy of New France stepped in and compelled the traders to carry their unwelcome passengers. On April 26, 1625, five Jesuits, Fathers Charles Lalemant, Ennemond Massé, Jean de Brébeuf and two lay brothers, joined the ship and set sail for New France. For two months at sea, the Fathers silently suffered the scorn and hostility of the officers and crew of the ship.

The ship reached Champlain's "Habitation" on June 15, but Champlain was absent in France, and the chief Huguenot trader at Quebec brusquely refused to allow the Jesuits to land. The entire population of Quebec had been poisoned by a slanderous and bitter attack against the newcomers, the Black Robes, and hostility bristled on every side. There seemed no choice for the Jesuits but to return to France on the same vessel.

Then a rowboat approached the ship, manned by two or three of the Récollet frères. Boldly they climbed aboard, warmly welcomed the Jesuits, assisted in transferring the baggage and ferried the Jesuits ashore. Not daring to use physical force, the scowling Huguenot traders could only look on as the first Jesuits to reach Quebec knelt and kissed the earth.

Huronia was on the lips and in the minds of the Jesuit Fathers from the moment they arrived. They heard of the courageous Viel, who had remained alone and isolated in far-off Huronia for more than a year. Brébeuf, a giant of a man physically as well as spiritually, wasted no time. Within a few days of his arrival he was on his way to Huronia. But at Three Rivers he received bad news. Viel was dead. He had been drowned when his canoe overturned in the wild rapids at Rivière des Prairies. The tragedy was not an accident. The Hurons had arranged it so that they could seize Viel's belongings.

Brébeuf was persuaded to wait until the following summer, 1626, before attempting to reach Huronia. He returned to the friendly Récollet mission house at Quebec, then immediately joined a group of Montagnais. In their winter camps he learned a great deal about Indian life and became accustomed to the hardships of the bush.

Things went well for the Jesuits that summer of 1626. Champlain returned from France with a grant of land for the Fathers, and an eighty-ton ship laden with tools, supplies and food. On board were two more Jesuit Fathers, Philibert Noyrot and Anne de Noüe, as well as a lay brother and twenty carpenters and workmen. While the Huguenot traders complained, plans were laid for a Jesuit headquarters at Point-aux-Lièvres on the St. Charles River, about a mile from Quebec.

Brébeuf did not even wait to see it started. With the newcomer, Father Nouë, and Daillon, a Récollet, he joined a trading party returning to Huronia. The journey was made safely, and the three priests reached the Huron village of Otoüacha on Penetanguishene Bay, then went on to Toanché where Viel had worked.

Here they found Viel's hut intact, and here they lived until October. Then, on October 18, Daillon set out for the country of the Neutral Indians to preach the word of God. This area—now containing Brantford, Hamilton, London and Windsor—was rich in tobacco and furs which were traded to the Hurons. Fearing that Daillon might encourage the tribe to deal directly with the French, the Hurons dispatched messages to the Neutrals denouncing Daillon as a sorcerer, and urging Neutral medicine-men to drive him away. Even at that early date, tribal politics used subterfuge to preserve trade. Daillon, threatened with death, was escorted back to Toanché under the protection of an armed Frenchman, sent to his aid by Brébeuf.

The Toanché mission continued using Viel's hut as its headquarters. The following summer, 1627, Father Nouë, who was old, found that he could no longer cope with the rigours and hardships of the wilderness. He returned to Quebec, leaving Brébeuf and Daillon to carry on. In the fall of 1628, Daillon left Huronia, and Brébeuf was alone. He laboured among the Hurons for another year, living under the same conditions as they did, eating the food they ate, watching their pagan rites, and seeking converts among them. In spite of their friendship, none became Christianized. In 1629, three years after his arrival in Huronia, Brébeuf was ordered to return, to Quebec. He arrived in July to find the colony and his Jesuit companions in a state of complete confusion. It had begun three years earlier in 1626, the year Brébeuf had departed for Huronia.

Father Lalemant, Superior of the Canadian mission, had realized that both colonizing and Christianizing were impossible with the Huguenots controlling New France. He succeeded in appealing to Cardinal Richelieu, the King's advisor, to suppress the Huguenots and annul their charter. Richelieu had formed a new company called the Company of New France, headed by himself. The charter stipulated that only Catholics could come to the new colony, and that the Company would defray the cost of all missions for the following fifteen years. With unlimited funds at its disposal and the full power of the Roman Catholic Church at its elbow, the new group made lavish plans to build a Catholic empire in the New World.

A highly exaggerated impres
of Quebec at the time o
capture by the Kirkes. By I.
Vianen, in Hennipin, 1

Prise de QUÉBEC par les Anglois

In 1627, the future of New France looked bright indeed. Father Lalemant had returned to France to assist in the preparations. By the following spring, a fleet of eighteen vessels had assembled at Dieppe, laden with supplies of food, building materials, guns, cannon, ammunition and powder. Scores of hopeful colonists crowded the ships; on one vessel were Father Lalemant and the Jesuit Father Paul Ragueneau.

But soon the dreams and ambitions of France in the New World were abruptly checked. War broke out between France and England. While the proud fleet of eighteen French merchantmen put out into the English Channel and headed west, a tough, hard-hitting flotilla of three English raiders sped ahead of them to Canada, charged with destroying everything French in the New World. The swift English ships were under the command of David Kirke, a fearless privateer.

He arrived in Canada first, hit Tadoussac like a battering ram, subdued all French resistance on the St. Lawrence, and isolated Quebec. When he demanded Quebec's surrender, the redoubtable Champlain bluffed him out of an attack. Since Kirke was now in control of the St. Lawrence, he was in no hurry to destroy Quebec. Instead he burned the captured Basque ships, set the post of Tadoussac on fire, and sailed eastward to intercept the eighteen French vessels bound for Canada.

It was a bold move, but the clumsy French merchantmen fell easy prey to the fast, staunchly built, well-manned English warships. In the Bay of Gaspé, Kirke captured the entire French fleet, shifted cargoes, crews and passengers onto eight of the largest ships, burned the ten smaller ones, and then set sail for England with his booty and prisoners. Once in England, Father Lalemant and Father Ragueneau regained their liberty and were allowed to return to France.

On this July day in 1629, as Brébeuf listened to the end of the tale, another powerful English fleet lay just a few miles down the St. Lawrence. Surrender was inevitable, and all anyone could do was await the outcome. On July 22nd Quebec was handed over to the English; about thirty men remained behind, but Champlain, Brébeuf and his Jesuit companions, and forty-five or more inhabitants were returned to France.

Here the Récollets and Jesuits watched anxiously as the fate of Canada lay in the balance. Peace was finally restored, and a treaty was in the making. For three years they waited until the Treaty of St. Germain-en-Laye gave back to France all the territory she had lost in the war.

The path to Huronia was once more open!

A
New
Beginning

On July 5, 1632, the first French vessel to sail the St. Lawrence River in three years reached Quebec. On board were the three Jesuits: Paul Le Jeune, the new Superior-General; faithful Anne de Nouë; and a lay brother, Gilbert Burel. They found Quebec in ruins and the old mission house on the St. Charles River partly destroyed. Work commenced at once to restore the colony.

In France, Champlain had been appointed Lieutenant-Governor of New France. In March, 1633, he sailed for Quebec with three ships and two hundred colonists. Among them were Brébeuf and Massé; two more Jesuits, Antoine Daniel and Ambrose Davost, were picked up at Cape Breton where they had gone the year before.

Arriving at Quebec on May 23, the Jesuits joined their companions already at the mission house and preparations were made to return to Huronia at the first opportunity. During the English occupation, the Hurons had stayed away from Quebec, but when they heard that Champlain was back, a fleet of 140 canoes laden with tobacco, furs and over 700 Indians arrived in July to greet their old friend.

The routine of the Indians' arrival was nearly always the same: the first day building huts, the second holding council with the French, the third and fourth bartering, the fifth day feasting and the sixth day departing at daybreak. At this particular council Champlain introduced Brébeuf, Daniel and Davost to the Hurons, and negotiations were made for the three priests to return to Huronia with the fur fleet. However, an Ottawa Indian, seeking to make trouble between the French and Hurons over an Algonkian held prisoner by Champlain, persuaded the Hurons not to transport the missionaries. The French, who could chance neither the closing of the Ottawa River by the Algonkians nor a break in their friendship with the Hurons, decided it was advisable to wait. The fathers reluctantly remained at Quebec where they worked among the Indians and studied the Huron language. The following summer of 1634, a Huron fur brigade finally consented to take them to old Huronia.

The journey proved to be a dangerous one. As the previous white men had suffered, so the Jesuits suffered throughout the 800-mile journey to Huronia. Crowded and hunched in a canoe so fragile that any shift of position was forbidden, they sat hour after hour, day after day with their faces pressed against the backs of foul-smelling Indians to avoid being hit by the paddles. More than fifty times they were forced to wade in raging currents, pushing and dragging the empty canoes, trying to avoid the boulders and sharp rocks. Brébeuf counted thirty-five tortuous portages. The priests' water-soaked cassocks chafed their legs and hindered their progress. Their sandled feet were soon bruised by the rocks and torn by branches. Often a portage required several trips of one, two or

25

three leagues and led through dense forest, damp with perpetual shade and odorous with decayed leaves and wood.

They watched for food caches of parched corn in birch-bark containers, hidden far from the trail or buried in the sand. As evening approached they looked for a good camp by the shore, where dry wood was at hand. Each had his task: one collected wood, one put up a flimsy shelter, one prepared the meal and one made the fire, revolving a pencil of wood in a wooden slot until the friction kindled the tinder.

The Jesuits could look forward to a lonely life and a lonely, perhaps even appalling, death. Yet they pushed on. Their canoes became separated. Brébeuf could speak a little Huron, but Daniel and Davost could only suffer in silence. Davost was robbed of part of his baggage, including most of the books and writing materials belonging to the three priests. By the time they reached their destination they were exhausted.

After thirty days of travel, Brébeuf was abandoned on the shores of a lonely bay. He set out for his old village of Toanché but found only ruins. Etienne Brûlé, one of Champlain's young men, had been murdered by the Indians, who had then deserted the village. A wide, well-worn path led Brébeuf to a new cluster of huts a few miles away where the inhabitants of Toanché had re-established themselves. This was the new village of Ihonatiria.

Toward the end of August, Daniel and Davost with their French attendants reached Huronia. The three missionaries now revived the Huron mission in the village of Ihonatiria, for Brébeuf considered it best to stay where he was well known.

By ancient Huron custom the whole village joined in building the residence, which Brébeuf called Saint-Joseph. It was thirty-six feet long and about twenty feet wide, made of strong sapling poles planted in the earth with the tops bent and lashed into an arch for the roof, and covered with over-lapping sheets of bark. The priests divided the dwelling into three parts: the first an anteroom for storage; the second a kitchen, workshop, dining room, living room, school room and bedroom; the third, the chapel. Two platforms ran along the sides of the middle apartment, four feet from the ground. On top they kept chests for clothing and vestments. Underneath they slept on sheets of bark or boughs covered with matting, using blankets of skins and garments. A rude mill and a clock completed the furnishings.

The Indians were constant visitors to see their meagre belongings, such as the magnifying glass, the prism, or the wonderful clock that told them to eat at twelve strokes and to leave at four strokes. They were also fascinated by the writing of the priests. Brébeuf commented in his journal:

All this serves to gain their affections and to render them more docile when we introduce the admirable and incomprehensible mysteries of our Faith; for the belief they have in our intelligence and capacity causes them to accept without reply what we say to them.

The Growing Mission

Mission work continued but with disheartening results. The Fathers gathered together the children of the village, teaching them the Pater Noster, the Ave, the Credo and the Commandments, then dismissing them with small presents of beads or prunes. Sometimes the elders were invited to a discussion on the doctrine, but when urged to adopt the Faith they always replied: "It is good for the French but we are another people with different customs." The Indians had strong religious beliefs of their own; yet doggedly the Fathers worked and visited among them, teaching the word of God.

By mid-summer of 1636 Brébeuf and his two companions were joined by five more Jesuit Fathers—François le Mercier, Pierre Pijart, Pierre Chastelain, Isaac Jogues and Charles Garnier—who brought the sad news that Champlain had died on Christmas Day, 1635.

The pestilence, or contagious fever, which from time to time broke out in the Huron towns now struck violently. With it came the smallpox. Its ravages were appalling, and the usual festive winter season became a season of mourning. Suicides were frequent. The Jesuits went from village to village ministering to the sick, offering a few raisins or sweetened water. No house was left unvisited, for everywhere was heard the wailing of the sick and dying. Having tended to the body, the priests addressed themselves to the soul, trying to convince the dying of the need for baptism in the Faith. In spite of all their efforts the Indians died by the thousands and the population was all but wiped out.

In 1637, Brébeuf decided that a new and more populous centre for the mission had to be found. He chose the village of Ossossané, about twelve miles to the south and a short distance inland from the shore of Nottawasaga Bay. Here a large residence was built for the Fathers; it was a cabin seventy feet long, half of which contained the chapel ornamented with crucifixes, religious vessels and ornaments. The mission was named La Conception. There were about fifty dwellings in the town, each containing eight to ten families with a surrounding fort of upright pickets ten feet high.

Leaving Chastelain, Pijart and Isaac Jogues to work with the dwindling population of Ihonatiria, Brébeuf and the other four Fathers—Daniel, Davost, Mercier and Garnier—moved to Ossossané early in 1637. The new chapel was the wonder of the countryside. Indians came from miles around to see the marvellous building. Many infants and dying adults had been baptized, but now an Indian chief in full health had been won over to the Faith and was baptized in this new chapel.

Still the pestilence raged unchecked, but a new note was detected. The Jesuits had awakened in the Hurons' mingled emotions of wonder, perplexity, fear, respect and awe. Now it was whispered that they had caused the pestilence against which the Hurons had no resistance, and which threatened to exterminate the nation. The medicine-men were quick to blame the missionaries for the epidemic and turn the Indians against Brébeuf and his companions.

Few today would question the courage or sincerity of the Jesuits, but the Indians cannot be blamed for resenting the newcomers who tried to persuade them to subscribe to a totally new type of worship, and at the same time infected them with terrible viruses. The medicine-men were desperately worried about their people dying from diseases which they rightly associated with the white men.

The Jesuits were shut out from village cabins, pelted with sticks and stones by the children, and threatened with death by the braves. Brébeuf had no illusions about the danger. He knew that something had to be done if he and his friends were to remain alive. He summoned the Indians to a farewell feast, boldly told them that he knew he and his companions were about to die, but warned them of the eternal punishment they would receive because of their resistance to God, and their abuse of His messengers.

Perhaps the Hurons realized that the friendship of the French was essential for trading purposes. Perhaps it was their strong sense of a host's duty toward his guest. Perhaps it was because courage was the greatest virtue among the Hurons. Whatever the reason, the Fathers were not killed. The threats and pestering ceased; the Fathers went about their work unharmed, preaching the gospel, caring for the sick and often baptizing the dying.

A year after Brébeuf had made his headquarters in Ossossané, the pestilence had killed almost all of the Indians in Ihonatiria. The village was little more than a collection of empty longhouses. It was useless to maintain a mission there any longer. Brébeuf sought a new centre and settled on a large Huron town, Teanaostaiaé, about fifteen miles north of the present city of Barrie. The Indian councils agreed to a mission residence; it was built and Brébeuf named it Saint-Joseph II to differentiate it from the first Saint-Joseph at Ihonatiria. In June, Chastelain, Pijart and Jogues, the three Fathers who had worked at Ihonatiria, moved to the new mission.

At Ossossané, in some ways the daily life of the Fathers was little different from that of the Indians. Their house always smelled of smoke; they sat on logs around the fire to eat their meals from a wooden platter; their food was sagamite and sometimes pumpkin, squash or corn on the cob in season. No salt was available. They read and studied by daylight or by the fire. Wax candles were for the altar only. They cultivated wheat for sacramental bread. Four or five drops of wine was all that was available for Mass. To the Indians who brought them food they gave in return cloth, knives, awls, needles and trinkets.

The life of the Fathers was regulated according to Jesuit rules. They rose at four, said Masses, made private devotions, read religious books and breakfasted until eight, at which time they admitted the Indians. When setting out to baptize and instruct, one Father had to remain in the house to guard their possessions. Each priest was assigned a certain number of houses in the village, sometimes as many as forty. These houses often had five or six fires with two families to each. Dinner was served at two o'clock with grace said in Huron. A chapter of the Bible was read aloud during the meal. At four or five o'clock the Indians were dismissed and the rest of the evening was spent in reading, writing, studying the Huron language, devotions or arranging the affairs of the mission.

In 1638 twelve artisans and labourers arrived from Quebec to build a wooden chapel. Here the Fathers kept their pictures and ornaments and in the winter kept fires burning for their converts, who numbered about sixty at that time.

It is hard to imagine the difficulties endured by the Jesuits as they went about their work. They tramped through the woods in the deep snow and bitter cold of winter wearing a single blanket for warmth. At the end of a journey was a longhouse, crowded and stinking, swarming with lice and fleas. The acrid smoke choked their lungs and reddened their eyes. There was no privacy and no familiar food.

In summer, the acrid smoke of winter was replaced by stuffiness and the stench of rotting garbage. Deer flies, black flies and mosquitoes feasted on their tender skin not immune to the poison.

Physical hardships were appalling, yet to these must be added the mental anguish the Fathers must have suffered. The torture of enemy prisoners went on in plain sight, as did the pagan dances and native religious ceremonies. Dreams were followed to the letter, even if they meant murder. The presence of the Jesuits made no difference, because the words and teachings of the priests had no substance without some practical example of a way of life different from the society so firmly established in Huronia.

Alone or in pairs, the Jesuits struggled day after day, sustained only by their love of God and their desire to spread the Gospel. Communication was limited until they had learned the language; hostility and mockery were frequent. Nowhere were they really secure; nowhere could they withdraw and refresh themselves. Faith is kept alive by companionship and congenial fellowship with others. This comradeship was essential to the dedicated and strange life led

Re-enactment of life within the Huron longhouse.

by the Jesuits in Huronia. They were separated from the Hurons by their European education and completely isolated from the relative civilization in Quebec.

This was the situation which confronted the new Superior, Father Jérôme Lalemant, brother of Charles Lalemant, who had led the first Jesuits to Quebec in 1625. Accompanied by Simon le Moyne and François du Peron, he reached Huronia late in the summer of 1638.

30

Lalemant had the organizing ability and practical views which Brébeuf—despite his enthusiasm, energy and courage—lacked.

Brébeuf's plan of having separate residences in the largest Huron towns was not working out well. The hard life he and the others were leading served no practical Christian purpose; it was self-sacrificing, but the Jesuits were not in Huronia to prove that they could live like savages. They were there to Christianize the Indians and to teach them a way of life which made better use of their lands, materials and crafts. Little progress had been made. In seven years, Brébeuf had baptized only one Huron in good health, but this had only served to increase the hostility of the medicine-men.

One of Lalemant's first acts was to send out his missionaries to take a house-by-house, fire-by-fire census of Huronia. It was found that there were thirty-two hamlets and villages, comprising in all about 700 houses, 2,000 fires and some 12,000 people. Lalemant travelled the wilderness, visiting numerous native villages and studying the extent and needs of the area and its people. He soon realized that some central headquarters for the missionaries had to be established if the work was to assume any real permanence. This would be a stronghold of the Faith from which the Fathers might go forth to minister, returning periodically for rest, relaxation and prayer. It would be an abode of reasonable comfort and safety.

Lalemant discussed the problem with Brébeuf, Daniel and the others. He wanted some centre which would not have to be abandoned every time a Huron village moved. It would have to be able to stand on its own, free of interference from any particular clan, but accessible to all. Especially, he wanted a centre of religious life comparable to the monasteries that had risen as focal points of spiritual life in medieval Europe.

The Site Is Chosen During the fall of 1638 and in the early months of 1639, Father Lalemant, advised and guided by Brébeuf and others who were familiar with the terrain of Huronia, searched out several possible locations, finally settling on a site in the heart of Huron country. It met every requirement. In his *Relations* of 1639-40 he writes: "The place is situated in the middle of the country, on the shore of a beautiful river, not more than a quarter of a league in length, which joins together two lakes. One, extending to the west and verging a little towards the north, might pass for a fresh-water sea; the other lies towards the south and has a contour of hardly less than two leagues."

Hurons called the river Isiaragui, now known as the Wye; the large lake was called Attigouantan, now Lake Huron; the smaller one was today's Mud Lake. The placid river emptied into Georgian Bay less than a mile north; streams led south from Mud Lake in every direction; access by water to Sainte-Marie was unobstructed. A stream flowed through the site and a free-flowing spring bubbled in the southern area. A network of Huron trails led to the village. Ossossané was only eight miles away; Saint-Joseph II, at Teanaostaiaé, was little more than twelve miles to the south-east.

With the site chosen, Father Lalemant immediately approached the Ataronchronons, a Huron tribe who lived in the area, and with presents secured the "right" to build there. No such thing as legal ownership of property existed, but the "right" to land was a solemn promise. The property on which Sainte-Marie rose was open Huron land. The question of its ownership was never even considered; Huronia was simply the land of the Hurons, a vast wilderness broken only by native villages, adjacent fields, a network of forest trails, rivers and lakes. The guttural agreement of a forgotten chieftain gave the Jesuits the privilege of using the land. The Fathers claimed no ownership but considered themselves guests in Huronia, rather than proprietors of even a foot of its soil.

A clearing was made near the river bank and the first building of Sainte-Marie was erected in the summer of 1639. It was a Huron-type longhouse, twenty feet by forty feet, with the sides parallel to the river some thirty feet away. Five French workmen built the house under the direction of Isaac Jogues. The longhouse was divided by a partition near one end to form a temporary chapel, while the remainder of the space lay open, with four cone-shaped fire-pits in the centre. The interior was primitively decorated and furnished.

While this first house of Sainte-Marie was under construction, Father Lalemant and six of the ten Jesuits in Huronia lived at nearby Ossossané, while Brébeuf and two others carried on at old Teanaostaiae. In the autumn of 1639, Father Lalement and his six companions moved from Ossossané to Sainte-Marie; in the spring of 1640 Brébeuf and his two associates joined them. Father Lalemant wrote in 1640:

And thus we have now in all the country, but a single house which is to be firm and stable, the vicinity of the waters being very advantageous to us for supplying the want, in these regions, of every other vehicle; and the lands being fairly good for the native corn, which we intend, as time goes on, to harvest for ourselves.

Having received the right to build, Father Lalemant and the other Jesuits must have soon started making plans for building their permanent mission which they called Sainte-Marie-among-the-Hurons. The result of their efforts and dedication was a truly amazing architectural and engineering achievement.

Since unfortunately there is no record of the actual building progress, we will have a clear idea of Sainte-Marie only by viewing it as it must have been at the height of its brief life. We can see this because of the work of Dr. Wilfrid Jury, who is largely responsible for the excavation and accurate reconstruction of the mission. Dr. Jury, Curator of the Museum of Indian Archaelogy, University of Western Ontario, discovered which building was which and where each was located. Because of rebuilding, we are able to visualize daily life at Sainte-Marie as it was more than three centuries ago.

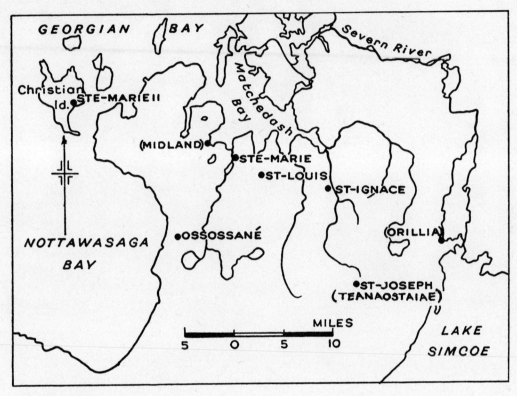

*Sainte-Marie and its
neighbourhood.*

An aerial view of Saint-Marie-Among-the-Hurons.

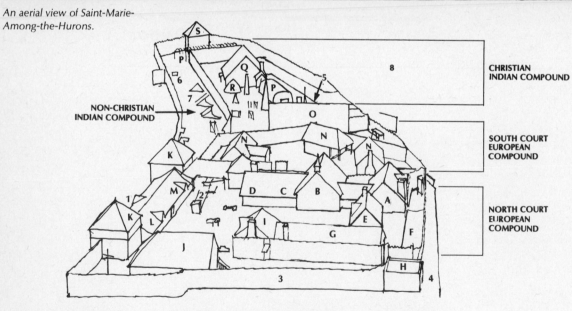

CHRISTIAN INDIAN COMPOUND

NON-CHRISTIAN INDIAN COMPOUND

SOUTH COURT EUROPEAN COMPOUND

NORTH COURT EUROPEAN COMPOUND

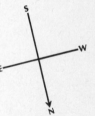

A Jesuit Dwelling	**H** North-west Bastion	**O** Indian Church	**2** Waterway
B Chapel	**I** Dwelling	**P** Huron Longhouse	**3** Palisades
C Carpenter Shop	**J** Granary	**Q** Hospital	**4** Pilgrim's Walk
D Blacksmith Shop	**K** Bastion	**R** Algonkian Wigwam	**5** Cemetery
E Cookhouse	**L** Barracks	**S** Five-sided Bastion	**6** Well
F Stable	**M** Storeroom		**7** Lean-to
G Barn	**N** Dwellings	**1** Gateway	**8** Wye River

PART THREE

SAINTE-MARIE
THE WILDERNESS
MISSION
1639-1649

From a hill to the north one can look down on a fort measuring 765 feet from north to south, completely surrounded by double palisades with bastions and lookouts placed at strategic points. From the square stone bastions in the north-west corner, watch could be kept on the River Wye and the water channel to the fort; the north-east corner juts out in a sharp lookout point which guards the only approach by land; the five-sided tower at the southern tip points into Indian country.

Inside the northern end of the fort are stone walls flanked with impregnable stone bastions. This is the completely self-sustaining European compound separated from the southern portion by double palisades and ditch-works. It is the most crowded part, and the buildings form two court-yards.

South of the ditch-works lies the area designated as the Indian compound. It contains few buildings, with one longhouse situated between the inner and outer palisades.

Approaching, one cannot help being impressed by the sturdy timber walls with clean, square corners. The French had searched the forests for tall, straight-grained, red cedar trees which they felled and split to a uniform size with their iron tools. The tops of the trees were burned and pointed before the bottoms were sunk into a two-and-a-half foot trench. An earth embankment completed the wall.

Sainte-Marie's main entrance is at the north end of the east wall and is flanked by a stone-walled building on the left and a timber-walled building on the right. Passing through a ten-foot-wide wood and stone entrance with massive timber gates, which swing up and out of the way on hinges, we find ourselves in a low-ceilinged passageway leading to the inner court. To the left and right of the passageway, in a windowless gloom, are Sainte-Marie's most invulnerable rooms.

Main Entrance

The main entrance to Sainte-Marie.

These are large rooms, about thirty-five feet wide and a good seventy-five feet long. The one on the right is presumed to have been a barracks which housed some twenty French soldiers sent to Sainte-Marie in the mid-1640's. Before their arrival it was probably used as a storage area; an analysis of its soil yields no evidence of a particular usage in ancient times. The outside wall of this portion of Sainte-Marie is not of stone but of heavy timbers. It has been concluded that at the time of its burning in 1649, Sainte-Marie was still being strengthened, and that this portion had yet to be walled with stone. Bearing out this conclusion was the discovery of a line of post-moulds—archaeological evidence of a timber palisade—which formed a fan-shaped protective wall around all of the stone portions of the mission. It seems likely that the builders of Sainte-Marie erected this outer, protective palisade to provide a temporary barrier while the work of building stone walls went on behind.

On the basis of chemical analysis of the earth which revealed a high saturation of animal oil, we assume that the room to the left of the passageway, identical in size to the barracks, was used for hanging skins and pelts to dry. Today a maze of saplings form primitive drying racks on which hang hides and pelts. Here too, on the sturdy cross-beams which span the room, are canoes made as they were in ancient times, using cedar strip for the framework, birch-bark for covering and spruce roots and spruce gum for sealing.

Bastions There are no openings in the outer walls of either building, but windows were cut to face the compound inside. The roofs are of thick, strong elm bark, overlapped like shingles. The most notable aspect of the entire structure is the extreme sturdiness of timbers, beams and supports. Both barracks and drying room join strong stone bastions at either end which have no openings except an arched entrance facing the inner compound. There are loopholes or slits to shoot through in the second story, which are positioned to sweep the eastern approach to the fort with musket fire.

Built of solid stone, about two-and-a-half feet thick, the two main bastions were impregnable to Indian attack. They extend beyond the barracks and drying room, and the upper story is well above the roofs of the buildings within the fort thus providing a constant lookout over the land.

The walls of the original bastions still showed above the earth a few feet when reconstruction began in 1964. Rather than mar these examples of early masonry, the present bastions were built around them, so that today you may see part of the actual walls of old Sainte-Marie, just as they were built by the mason, Pierre Tourmente.

There is one bastion which stands well inside the compound. Why it was constructed is not known, but it is presumed that the

The outer east wall and bastions.

original plan of Sainte-Marie called for a complete stone-wall enclosed area with bastions at each corner. This plan was probably abandoned as Sainte-Marie grew in stature and stout timber palisades came to encircle its three acres.

All through Sainte-Marie, few field stones appear in the construction. This was because there is little field stone in the immediate vicinity of the mission. The walls, foundations and fireplaces are built of trimmed grey limestone brought from what is now Port

McNicol, three miles away. This was a tremendous effort which involved quarrying the stones, hauling them to the lake, transporting them by raft or boat, and finally trimming and placing them in mortar.

North Court Beyond the entrance passageway is the north court of the European Compound. This was the hub of life at Sainte-Marie. Here are built the cookhouse, the carpenter and blacksmith shops, the dwellings and the chapel.

In the north-east corner of Sainte-Marie stands a tall cross, some twenty-five feet high, surrounded by a row of pickets. Similar crosses rise in each corner of Sainte-Marie.

The granary also is located in this north-east area. It has an overhanging "porch" where corn stalks are stored on a lattice-work of poles. Additional bins and racks provide storage for corn, grain, sunflower pods, roots and vegetables. In Sainte-Marie as it exists today, the granary backs onto a small compound, which leads to the north-west bastion, close to the banks of the Wye River. This is the only part of Sainte-Marie not in its original position. During excavations, it was found that this bastion once stood where railroad tracks now lie. It was impractical to do more than reconstruct it as close to the original position as possible. Inside this bastion, we can

A view of the north court looking north. The granary is on the right, and to the left is a dwelling, possibly occupied by Charles Boivin.

look across the river to what must have been the fields of Sainte-Marie.

Along the west palisades facing the Wye River is an open pathway. This is called Pilgrim's Walk and it provides access to Jean de Brébeuf's grave in the Indian Mission Church in the south compound.

Why the builders of Sainte-Marie erected inner palisades to separate certain areas is not known, but they probably felt that a number of small areas, fortified by timber walls, would be easier to defend than one large open space. The compound at the back of the granary, for instance, is simply an area enclosed by the strong outer palisades and an inside palisade running nearly parallel to it. This may have been a work area for builders, stone masons and other workmen.

From the northwest bastion we return to the main compound and the European-type buildings. There is a small building, a little to the right of the main entrance. It seems possible that Charles Boivin, master builder of Sainte-Marie, once lived here, for its privacy indicates that it was the home of someone who needed to work, study and plan without interruption. Today it is designated as his dwelling and is furnished as it might have been 300 years ago.

The fireplace in this building is narrow, high and deep. To the left of the door are a table and bench, both constructed without the use of a single nail. Shelves and a cupboard with hinges and latches, all made of wood, line the nearby wall. An ancient iron chest rests on top of the cupboard, and a broom made of twigs leans in one corner.

Across the room is a work bench; lying on it or hanging on wall-pegs are small saws, an old measuring wheel, compasses of both wood and metal, small mallets, chisels, a brace and bit, hammers and wooden planes. An unfinished model of a building stands on the bench, for Charles Boivin always made an accurate model of anything he was going to construct. Hanging from the ceiling is an exact copy of a seventeenth-century French lantern from Normandy.

Stairs lead to the second story. Hand-made beds, lined with fragrant cedar boughs and covered with blankets and furs, plus a small table and chair are the only objects in the room. A narrow, high-pitched gable, pushing out through the elm bark roof, is shuttered for protection against rain and snow.

The wood of the buildings and furnishings at Sainte-Marie is exceptionally thick because only the broad-axe, adze and pit-saw were used to make the lumber. With these instruments it was very difficult to fashion thin boards.

Immediately west of Boivin's dwelling is Sainte-Marie's barn. **Barn** Who lived in tiny living-quarters at the east end of this building, under the same roof but otherwise separated by a passageway?

side a north court dwelling.

In a building designated as the
residence of Charles Boivin,
master builder, this model
recreates his methods. He always
made a model of any structure he
designed and built.

The fireplace in the dw
attached to the barn is bu
its original founda

Certainly it was someone skilled in looking after livestock, for he was within earshot of a roomy box-stall where calves were born. A small fireplace, table, bench and small cupboard furnish this tiny living cubicle. Shelves with hang-up pegs flank the fireplace; wooden vessels, such as a water flagon made from a small tree trunk, lie about.

Across the passageway is the barn itself. Poles enclose the box-stall, with the feeding manger made from saplings. The poles are held in place by hide thongs. Just outside the box-stall, the primitive tools of this first Canadian farm lie about: rakes made entirely of wood, forks using the natural prongs of a tree for tines, big storage vessels made from hollowed out tree trunks, twig brooms, and shovels made from one piece of wood. The floor is of packed earth. Rows of corn and sunflowers hang drying from the ceiling and above the ceiling is a roomy hayloft. Outside, the hayloft overhangs the ground floor providing a sheltered feeding area as well as allowing a pole chute to descend from the loft. Here there are water troughs of hollowed logs, primitive tools hanging on wall pegs and a hay-carrying rack, its frame made of poles and its base made of deerskin laced to the sides.

Saint-Marie's barn housed cattle, swine and poultry. The section at the right was living quarters possibly those of the man in charge of the livestock.

The hay-loft of Sainte-Marie's barn.

44

The bull's stall in the barn. Corn
hangs drying from the ceiling.

Stable To the right of the barn are the stables which flank the west palisades by the river bank. The heavy roof, covered with sand as protection against fire, provided warm shelter for the animals and also served as a sentry walk and firing platform. The long, narrow stables are in their original location. It was established that the building was a stable when an analysis of the earth proved that manure and urine had once mixed with the soil in large quantities. Near the entrance is a solid log box-stall, probably used to house the bull. Next to this is one of two chicken-coops made with interwoven alder branches. Several stalls, floored with split poles, extend along the wall.

A work and feeding area at one end of Sainte-Marie's barn.

The land around Sainte-Marie was fertile and the farming was **Agriculture** undoubtedly done in the flat fields beyond the far shore of the Wye River. In addition, it is possible that small gardens existed between the inner and outer palisades. Some planting must have been done at once, because in 1641 Father Garnier writes: "On the feast of St. Joseph, our patron, we saw our house provided with corn for a year." Where the native corn, the pumpkin or the staple bean originally came from is a secret of nature, but one of the most amazing sights to greet the first whites in Huronia was the great two-mile-long fields of tall, lush corn, laden bean stalks and sprawling beds of yellow pumpkins. We may assume that corn, as well as sunflowers, pumpkins, squash and beans were all indigenous to the area and formed the staple crops of Sainte-Marie.

The soil of the Huronia region is sandy and requires frequent rain to be productive. But seldom did a season pass without a good crop; the Hurons were wise in the ways of the weather and always planted enough corn to last two, three or four years. If the planting yielded a large crop, the surplus corn was traded with other tribes. It is likely that the white farmers followed the Huron's example, for in 1649 a three-year surplus was at hand. It is also likely that they followed the Huron's method of soaking some of the seeds before planting and fertilizing the ground with fish.

It is possible that the Jesuits took advantage of the wild fruits such as the strawberries, raspberries, blueberries, acorns, cherries and edible roots that grow in the area to add variety to the diet at Sainte-Marie. They may also have gathered wild plums. These were buried in the ground to sweeten, for wild plums have an unpleasantly sharp taste until touched by frost.

Sainte-Marie was not without meat. Heifers, calves, bulls, swine and poultry once thrived there, but there is no evidence of sheep. It was a colossal task to bring animals 800 miles from Quebec by canoe or raft over some fifty portages! Father Ragueneau wrote in 1649:

We have larger supplies from fishing and hunting than formerly; and we have not merely fish and eggs, but also pork, and milk products and even cattle, from which we hope for great addition to our store... no blight of evil has fallen upon us; nay, we have enough provisions upon which to live comfortably during three years.

Long before Sainte-Marie was established, the French had been successful in growing staple European crops. At Quebec crops such as wheat, rye, oats, hemp, barley, peas, beans, turnips, radishes, carrots, parsnips, cabbages and a wide variety of culinary herbs had been grown successfully. Apple trees and grape vines also flourished. There is mention of pear trees, cucumbers, squash and even lettuce. It is reasonable to believe that most or all of these reached Sainte-Marie in the form of either seeds or cuttings, and that Masson, the gardener, would plant such a variety in the fields and gardens.

From Ossossané, in 1638, comes the first record of a crop being harvested by white men west of Quebec city. Le Mercier wrote in June: "... the harvest was about a half-bushel of good wheat, which was large for the little we sowed; a small keg of wine, which kept very well during the entire winter, and is still passably good."

Central Cookhouse The central cookhouse where all the food was prepared is one of the most interesting buildings in Sainte-Marie. Standing almost in the centre of the west side of the court, it is entered through a Dutch door. This is a door built in two sections so that the upper section may be opened for light and air while the lower one remains closed. From 1645 on, Ambroise Brouet was the official cook. Food prepared in the cookhouse was carried at meal times to the various dwellings, Jesuit residence, hospital and other quarters for there was no central dining place.

The cookhouse, centrally located in the European Court.

In the reconstructed cookhouse, the cook's bunk
has been placed beside the fireplace.

The cookhouse is constructed of two rows of horizontal planking filled with rocks and clay for insulation. These planks begin at least eighteen inches to two feet below the ground and are supported by upright posts at intervals of ten to twelve feet. This type of construction is known as "colombage pierotté". Below the cookhouse floor there is a cellar eighteen feet long, six feet wide and six feet deep which is entered by a trap door. The walls are lined with cedar logs. Pine flooring two inches thick lies over a fine layer of white sand.

The chief point of interest in the cookhouse is the huge fireplace with its adjoining bakeoven built on its original foundations. Beside the fireplace is a bunk bed, a common building feature in the 1600's. Ambroise Brouet must have slept here, since his duties often woke him as early as four a.m. Close by is a broad, waist-high work table, dusty with corn meal; on top are wooden dishes containing the meal, with wooden grinding pestles and spoons scattered about. Leaning against the bakeoven are long-handled, shovel-like tools made from one piece of wood. They were used to place the loaves in the oven which is about six feet deep and to retrieve the finished loaves.

On the far wall, rows of shelves hold many wooden vessels needed to prepare food—bowls, plates, platters and mugs, all hewn from logs. Indian baskets are scattered about. In the fireplace is an old French pot-hanger suspended directly over the fire, with notches allowing various heights for different cooking purposes.

From a maze of poles on the ceiling hang clusters of corn, sunflower pods, sage and tobacco. Sainte-Marie's cooks followed the Huron practice of picking corn at harvest time, then turning up the leaves around the ears and hanging the bundles in rows along the roofs of their longhouses. When the grain was dry, it was shelled, cleaned and put into large bark casks.

Many valuable artifacts were found in the cookhouse cellar: a beautiful blue-green Venetian glass vessel, three and a half inches high, eight pieces of lead of unrecognizable shape, five pieces of copper and seven segments of iron, four knives, one fork and a fish hook, one rosary bead, four buttons, two leather shoe soles and several pieces of shattered glass. Indian remains consisted of one celt or stone hammer, one gaming stone, three trade beads, eight pottery fragments and nineteen pipe fragments. "Most abundant, however, were bones of cows, pigs, wapiti, woodchuck and chickens distributed throughout the fill of the cellar. All bones had been boiled and were usually sawn. In the central area of the cellar were deposits of egg-shell, shattered and densely packed in ashes . . . larger still were the deposits of fish bones and fish scale."

Work in the cookhouse began early with the boys up first to replenish fires and carry wood to the fireplace. Then the stables were opened, cows were milked and driven to pasture where lush grass and cool water kept them sleek and fat. The swine were fed kitchen leftovers fortified with corn; kernels were strewn for the clucking hens and crowing roosters. Before the sun was properly up, the animals were tended for the day. Then came breakfast, and after that a quick dispersal to duties. Ambroise Brouet and his two helpers tidied up the breakfast and began preparations for the noon meal.

Most trays, platters and other utensils used at Sainte-Marie were probably fashioned from wood. Here are knives, forks, spoons and serving dishes.

work table in the cookhouse, with wooden vessels in racks
ond and drying corn hanging from the roof.

A corner of the cookhouse showing wooden buckets, copper vessels and a twig broom.

*The cookhouse with its variety of
wooden utensils.*

To the right of the cookhouse is a row of buildings which form the **Blacksmith's Shop** south side of the court. They are connected to each other and present a varied and attractive façade. Closest to the main entrance is the blacksmith's shop.

There was no busier spot than this shop, where brother Ludovicus Gauber, a master craftsman, toiled from morning until night making scores of things from iron: hammers, chisels, knives, punches, gimlets, wedges, awls and augers for the carpenters; hoes, spades and tools for the gardeners; hinges, locks, catches, handles, keys and clasps for the builders; every spare minute was used for making nails, hundreds of which were found during excavations. These vary in length from half an inch to eight inches and have flat heads and square shanks. Gauber would also be called upon to mend guns.

The blacksmith also made axes specifically for native trade. Although these were inferior to the European broad-axes they would certainly have been better than the old stone ones. They were made by folding back the band thus forming a heavy head in which a wooden handle was placed.

Prominent in the European Compound is the Jesuit chapel, with its spire and weathercock. To the immediate left are the carpentry and blacksmith shops, and to the right, Jesuit dwellings. In the foreground is stonework from buildings that have not been reconstructed.

blacksmith shop, with smithy tools and anvil.

The forge in the blacksmith's shop is reconstructed on its original foundation. It is of just the right height to permit lifting iron from the fire to the anvil. The fire-pit is about four feet square, but the actual fire which heated the metal would be no more than a few inches across, a small, concentrated, extremely hot fire. Charcoal or hemlock bark was probably used for fuel.

The bellows, which provided a forced draught beneath the fire, are located high on the side of the stone forge, with a duct down through the masonry and then up the fire area. The bellows in the reconstructed Sainte-Marie were secured in France, and are typical of the period. They resemble a large accordian, built into a sturdy wooden frame, and operated by a pulleyed thong which hangs down within easy reach of the blacksmith.

The anvil is mounted on a large log close to the forge. The one we see today is a seventeenth century anvil purchased in France. The anvil has hardly changed its essential shape in over one thousand years. It has a spreading base with a rectangular face where most of the smith's work is done, and a tapered beak over which pieces of iron can be curved for rings, links and shackles. The height of the anvil from the ground is very important since it must be exactly suited to the smith. The position of the anvil in relation to the fire also is carefully chosen. It must be close enough so that the heated iron does not cool as it is swung from fire to anvil.

A water cask, made from a large, hollowed log sits nearby. This is kept full of water in which the smith douses the hot iron for tempering. Another essential item is the tongs with which the smith handles the red-hot iron.

The blacksmith shop, showing the forge, bellows, anvil and quenching tub made from a log.

Carpenter's Shop Just as busy as Louis Gauber was Charles Boivin, builder and architect of Sainte-Marie. His carpenter shop was identical in size to the blacksmith shop and adjoining it. Carpenters and wood workers played a most important role, for wood was used for hundreds of purposes. The restored carpenter shop is furnished with tools of the seventeenth century, most of which were secured in France. Stacks of planking and logs are piled about and on a work bench lie felling axes, broad-axes, planes, chisels, hammers and mallets. Nearby stands a shaving horse, a device which the craftsman sat on and which held the wood secure while it was shaped with a draw-knife. A home-made grindstone and wheelbarrow also are among the fittings. Half-finished bed ends, door hinges, clasps and shutter fastenings, pestles, dishes and other vessels show how various work was done.

The carpenter shop, with its wooden vise and woodworking tools.

d workmanship of the
·nter is apparent at the apex
: five-sided timber bastion.

In the Sainte-Marie carpenter shop is a pit-saw, the tool used to cut out planks and lumber from large timber. The method is age-old and was used in many countries. A squared timber was placed on trestles about seven feet above the ground. Two sawyers were required. One stood on top of the timber, the other stood on the ground. They sawed in a lengthwise direction along the timber. The man on top pulled the saw up, the one below pulled it down to complete the cutting stroke. A drawn line guided the workers, but each cut was stopped a little short of the end so that the top sawyer would have something to stand on until the last cut was made. These rough pine and cedar planks were often finished by plane.

The architecture of Sainte-Marie required many eleven-by-eleven-inch timbers which had to be hewn and brought to the site. The hardwood came from the higher slopes of Mud Lake, the soft woods from the marshy land of the valleys. The logs were squared with an ordinary felling axe. An expert seventeenth century craftsman could completely square a sixteen-foot timber in about two hours. After roughly squaring the log, he would finish it off with his broad-axe, and if it were to be exposed, the surface was carefully dressed with an adze, a very sharp, hoe-shaped chisel with a wooden handle. It was a dangerous tool to use because the craftsman stood on his work and cut towards his toes!

A typical cupboard of Sainte-Marie, made without nails and with a sliding door.

The European chapel in winter.

European Chapel   Adjoining the carpenter shop is the private church dedicated to the Blessed Virgin. This was used for the Fathers' devotions as well as services for the Europeans. The church is floored with pine planks, with the altar at one end. There is no fireplace so warmth is provided by braziers, and there are no pews. Religious objects adorn the altar. Hanging from the cross-beams is a seventeenth century sanctuary lamp. The outside appearance of the chapel is impressive. Its tower, topped by a cross and then a weather-cock, is the highest point in Sainte-Marie. The bell which today hangs in the steeple was secured in France and dates back to 1648. The exposed gable ends combined with the outside wall-support timbers form a strong pattern above the wide entrance door. The chapel is a fine example of craftsmanship. Its roof, like many others in Sainte-Marie, is of cedar strips.

Jesuits' Residence   Adjoining the chapel is the Jesuit residence where the Fathers and lay brothers lived when not out on missions. The dining room is immediately off the chapel. It is sparsely furnished with tables and benches, shelves containing wooden vessels and a few religious objects on the walls. It was here the Jesuits ate their meals, brought to them from the cookhouse across the way.

Interior of the Jesuit residence, showing hand-made table, benches and cupboard.

Next to the dining room is the larger Jesuit common room containing a large fireplace, curved table and matching curved benches, a settee made of wood, wall shelves and with corn husk mats scattered on the floor. At the rear of the room are the sleeping quarters of the Superior and his Assistant; a consultation room is on the far wall. Sliding doors shut off these rooms. Low beds with stretched skin mattresses, blankets and bear-skin coverings, a few stools, wall pegs and a small cupboard complete the austere furnishings.

Up a stairway, on the second story, are the sleeping cubicles for the Fathers and a dormitory for the lay brothers. A back stairway leads outside to the ground and into the south court.

Sleeping Quarters

A corner of the Jesuit common room.

boards and the stairway to sleeping quarters above.

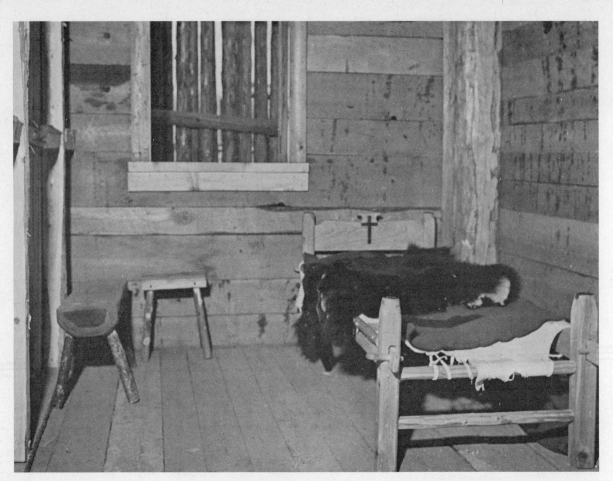

The Superior's quarters.

Sturdy stairs lead from the common room of the Jesuit residence to the sleeping quarters above.

A Priest's cell in the Jesuit residence.

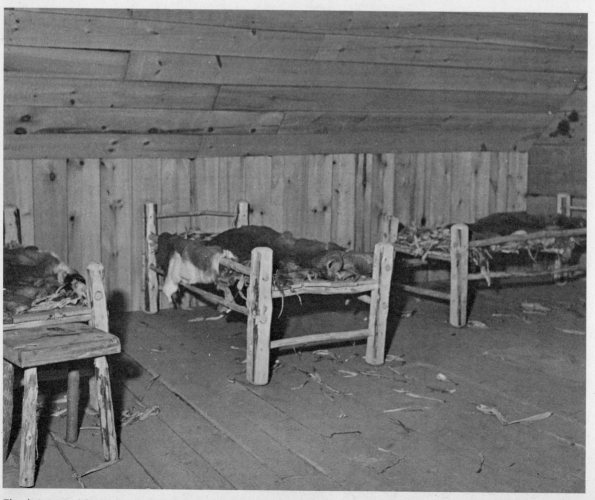

The dormitory of the lay brothers, upstairs over the common room.

Waterway   Between the north and south courts of Sainte-Marie is a waterway that archeologists have concluded was a lock-canal. This is probably the most astonishing of all the features at Sainte-Marie and the first to be discovered in North America. It leads from the Wye River through the very heart of Sainte-Marie to a point near the main entrance. Who engineered this amazing structure will probably never be known. It begins with an aqueduct which feeds the water system inside the fort from springs in the hills to the north. This aqueduct enters Sainte-Marie through the north-east corner, joining the waterway almost opposite the north-east bastion. It then becomes navigable just opposite the stone wall of the barracks, where it has a uniform width of four feet, quite wide enough to allow free passage of large Indian canoes or even longboats.

This section runs north and south, paralleling the stone walls of the barracks and drying room. A few feet beyond the south-west main bastion, it turns sharply west toward the river. The corner is enlarged to permit craft to easily make the turn. The channel then continues west until it meets a roomy landing basin. At the outlet of the basin is a lock-gate which could be raised or lowered to change the water levels up or down to match the level in the next lock, a few yards below.

This second lock is also flanked by a loading basin, separated from the waterway by timber pilings and planks. The channel continues to the third and final lock before the water gate leading to the open river. The entire waterway is lined with timbers and some sections are floored with planks.

A loading basin of the waterway in the European south compound.

How did the waterway system work?

In a canoe, we enter through the water gate on the River Wye and into the first lock. The gate is lowered as soon as we are safely inside, thus preventing the water, which continually flows from above, to escape into the river. The second lock is opened, and gradually the basin in which we wait fills up. Our canoe slowly rises above the river behind us, until our level matches the level in the second lock. We paddle past this lock, which is at once lowered. Again, the next lock is opened, and the same thing happens; the waterway between the first and second locks fills, until we float on the same level as the water in the next lock. We paddle through the lock, which is immediately lowered, and we are now in the main waterway where we can paddle to within a few feet of the front entrance!

The waterway undoubtedly saved the builders of Sainte-Marie immense labour. Tons of stone were required to build bastions, walls and fireplaces. Hundreds of immense timbers were brought to Sainte-Marie for building purposes, and heavy crude iron must have come by canoe from far-off Quebec. The water route, which was the only means of transportation, leads directly through areas where stone walls were raised. It is also adjacent to the carpentry and blacksmith shops.

The excavation of the waterway proved invaluable in the overall reconstruction of Sainte-Marie, because here a wide variety of material was found that had escaped the flames which destroyed the rest of the mission. Elm bark was found in large quantities which established the fact that the roofs had been shingled with bark. It was learned from partially burned timber what type of material had been used, the width and breadth of the planks and boards, and the particular tools that had prepared the timber. From the nails, nailholes and shape of various remnants, specific details of construction were discovered. Enough remains of old gables were found to determine the pitch of the roofs.

In addition to the main waterway, there was a second water system which supplied fresh drinking water to the mission. This was a square timber flume which entered the fort almost alongside the granary and which carried water from the springs to the fort compound.

Sainte-Marie's waterway which led from the Wye River to the heart of the mission.

Gradually the population of Sainte-Marie increased. In 1644 there were thirty-six permanent residents. By 1647 this number had grown to forty-two, and in 1648 had reached sixty-six. At some point in the mid-1640's, the Governor of New France sent soldiers to protect the Huron fur flotillas against Iroquois attack; it is recorded that "22 soldiers were lodged in our own house in Huronia, and ate at our own table."

While the master builder had his quarters in the north court, it is believed that the dwellings of the workers, boys and *donnés* were located in the sourth court of the European compound. This building differs in construction from all the other European buildings at Sainte-Marie. It is built with walls of upright logs and chinked with ground limestone mortar mixed with moss. It is double shuttered: the outside shutters slide back in channels while the inside shutters are hinged at the top and so swing down to close. This structure contains a large fireplace, built on its original foundations. At one side of the fireplace are two bunks, shielded by sliding doors which could completely isolate the occupants from the chatter and talk which undoubtedly went on in the common area. There are cupboards in the room, corn-husk mats near the hearth and a wood barrow. Tables and benches, big chests and a unique stump-seat carved from the base of a tree, are also part of the furnishings. The upstairs is devoted entirely to bedrooms for the men, and differs little from the cubicles in the Jesuit residence.

This structure (in the south court) with upright logs is a reconstruction of what is believed to have been the first European-style building in Sainte-Marie.

Corner of a dwelling in the south court. Note the sleeping bunks next the fireplace.

The other two dwellings in the south court revert to the timber-and-insulation type of wall construction. In one building is a cobbling centre for Jacques Levrier and Christopher Regnault, the two cobblers. In this room are a cobbler's bench, a hide-scraping device and the usual table, benches, shelves and tools.

The tailors at Sainte-Marie were Brother Dominique Scott, from 1640 to 1645, and Brother Peter Masson, from 1646 to 1649. The remaining building of the south court is designated as the possible tailoring centre. A wooden wash basin and clothes-board is at one wall, a toboggan and replicas of ancient Huron game sticks lean in one corner, and there are the usual cupboards, table and benches found in nearly all of Sainte-Marie's European style buildings.

The whole European compound was surrounded by palisades and

a ditch to strengthen the defences. From a point in the palisade was a three-foot square escape tunnel completely lined with timber, which ran sixty-five feet to the river bank. Through it a runner could be dispatched for help, or the inhabitants could escape in time of siege or fire.

The French went about their daily affairs living in comparative comfort within their palisades. Pierre Masson cultivated his gardens and fields. Louis Gauber, with sparks flying, shaped iron at his anvil. Dominique Scott, the tailor, cut and sewed new clothes or mended old ones, assisted by Masson in the winter. Charles Boivin, master-builder, and his crew chopped and sawed at a pile of long straight logs making timbers for new buildings. Pierre Tourmente, the stone mason, tapped at a slab of granite to be fitted into the base of a new bastion. The staccato rap of cobblers' hammers sounded from the bench of Jacques Levrier as he fashioned footwear for his busy

A dwelling in the south court of the European Compound.

companions. And the curious Hurons swarmed over Sainte-Marie, wondering at white men's ways, marvelling at the pigs and chickens, howling with laughter at milking time, but avoiding the glowing forge in the blacksmith shop which they believed was the fire of demons.

Life was hard during the first months at Sainte-Marie and food supplies ran low during the winter. In 1640, reinforcements arrived and by the autumn there were twenty-eight people, thirteen priests, one lay brother, six *donnés*, four youths and four workmen. The **Donnés** *donnés* were laymen who served the mission without pay. They were under no religious vows but were so dedicated to serving the Jesuits that they were willing to leave the comfort of their homes in France to accompany the priests on their mission to the Hurons; many were skilled workmen.

THE HURON CAROL

Father Jean de Brébeuf is believed to have written this carol in the Huron language for his Indian converts, as an interpretation of the Nativity. The translation is by J. E. Middleton, written in 1926. Gitchi Manitou means "Lord of all the world".

'Twas in the moon of winter-time,
When all the birds had fled,
That mighty Gitchi-Manitou
Sent angel choirs instead;
Before their light the stars grew dim,
And wondering hunters heard the hymn.

Jesus your King is born,
Jesus is born,
In excelsis gloria.

Within a lodge of broken bark
The tender Babe was found,
A ragged robe of rabbit skin
Enwrapped His beauty 'round;
But as the hunter braves drew nigh,
The angel song rang aloud and high.

The earliest moon of winter-time
Is not so round and fair
As was the ring of glory on
The helpless Infant there.
The chiefs from far before Him knelt
With gifts of fox and beaver-pelt.

O children of the forest free,
O sons of Manitou,
The Holy Child of earth and heaven
Is born today for you.
Come kneel before the radiant Boy
Who brings you beauty, peace and joy.

*A dwelling in the south court,
near the waterway.*

These men played a major part in building and maintaining Sainte-Marie over its entire ten-year existence. One of them, Robert le Coq, was a business agent for the mission, covering the long dangerous route from Quebec to Sainte-Marie year after year, and looking after all supplies and goods. His declaration of servitude has been preserved:

I have given myself to the Society of Jesus to serve and assist with all my power and diligence the Fathers of the said Society . . . in such method and dress as shall be required . . . without claiming anything else whatever except to live and die with the said Fathers in whatever part of the world I am required to be with them; leaving to their free disposition all that concerns me and may belong to me.

The Jesuits in their turn drew up a similar agreement on behalf of the *donnés*:

We by these presents, accept him (Jean Guerin) as Donné in the capacity of a Domestic Servant during his lifetime . . . promising, on our part, to maintain him according to his condition with food and clothing, without other wages or claims on his part, and to care for him kindly in case of sickness, even to the end of his life, without being able to dismiss him, in such case, except with his own consent; provided that, on his part, he continues to live in uprightness, diligence and fidelity to our service.

Generally the *donnés* attended to the daily requirements, leaving the priests and lay brothers free for their religious duties. The youths at Sainte-Marie served under the *donnés* for a period of apprenticeship which eventually led to them becoming *donnés* themselves. Many of these *donnés* travelled new routes by land, and over lakes and rivers. They became expert canoemen, mixed with the natives, learned their language and their ways, and some of them later gave invaluable service to the governors of New France.

The spiritual life of the Jesuits was strictly regulated. Here at Sainte-Marie the monastic routines were virtually the same as those attempted under the primitive conditions of the old mission hut at Ossossané. Often only one or two priests were at hand in Sainte-Marie to carry out these monastic duties. Recalling Father Jérôme Lalemant's conception of Sainte-Marie as a central residence explains this situation. No more than once or twice a year did all the Jesuits meet at Sainte-Marie, and then only briefly for spiritual and physical refreshment.

Most of the Fathers' time was spent in the regional mission centres in the field. There were Ossossané, with twelve smaller settlements nearby, Cahiagué on Lake Simcoe with two additional villages, and finally Teanaostaiaé with two satellite missions, Saint-Michel and Saint-Ignace.

In pairs and accompanied by their lay attendants, the priests left Sainte-Marie for months at a time. Many trips were made in the bitter winter when the men were home from trading, fishing and hunting.

The mission of Sainte-Elisabeth was established for the Algonkians, who, driven by famine and fear of the Iroquois, often sought refuge in Huron country during the winter. Then there was Saint-Esprit for the Nipissings and other tribes east and north-east of Lake Huron, and Saint-Pierre for the tribes at the outlet of Lake Superior and the surrounding wilderness. The Jesuits built a mission on Manitoulin Island and also taught on the Bruce Peninsula.

Garnier and Joques went among the Petuns and Neutrals where Saint-Jean and Saint-Matthias had been founded while the first stone walls of Sainte-Marie were slowly rising. They met with extreme hostility and barely escaped with their lives. A year after Sainte-Marie had been established, Brébeuf and Chaumonot visited nineteen towns in the Neutral Nation, near Lakes Ontario and Erie, only to find that the wily Huron medicine-men were already there, inciting the Neutrals to kill the priests.

But the work went on.

*Interior of
a Huron longhouse
showing the raised platforms
which run the entire length
of the structure.*

Indian Compound   With the physical growth and security of Sainte-Marie came a most rewarding response from the hundreds of Indians who visited the mission. In planning Sainte-Marie the Fathers and their artisans conformed to the custom of providing a separate place for visitors. Even the smallest Huron village had an area set aside for visitors where they could stay in huts, cook their own food and keep their belongings. The Fathers built separate compounds for Christian and Indians not yet baptized. The Christian Indians occupied a large area south of, and separated from, the European south court. They were also separated by timber palisades from the unbaptized Indians who occupied the area between the inner and outer palisades. Here the Indians lived much as they did in their own villages with cabins, longhouses and temporary shelters dotting the area.

This authentic reconstruction of a Huron longhouse stands in the the compound set aside for Christian Indians.

Father Brébeuf in his *Relations* of 1635 had this to say about the Huron longhouse:

I cannot better express the fashion of the Huron dwellings than to compare them to bowers or garden arbours, some of which, in place of branches and vegetation, are covered with cedar bark, some others with large pieces of ash, elm, fir or spruce bark; and, although the cedar bark is best, according to common opinion and usage, there is, nevertheless, this inconvenience, that they are almost as susceptable to fire as matches. There are cabins or arbours of various sizes, some two brasses [about eleven feet] in length, others of twenty, or thirty or forty; the usual width is about four brasses, their height about the same. There are no different stories; there is no cellar, no chamber, no garret. It has neither window nor chimney, only a miserable hole in the top of the cabin, left to permit the smoke to escape.

If you go to visit them in their cabins . . . you will find there a miniature picture of Hell, seeing nothing, ordinarily, but fire and smoke, and on every side naked bodies, black and half roasted, mingled pell mell with the dogs, which are held as dear as the children of the house, and share beds, plates and food of their master. Everything is in a cloud of dust, and if you go within, you will not reach the end of the cabin before you are completely befouled with soot, filth and dirt. Fleas are in clouds. The smoke sometimes grounded all of us who were in the cabin, that is, it caused all of us to place our mouths against the earth in order to breath.

However, the Hurons were not the only visitors to Sainte-Marie. The Algonkians came too. Unlike the Hurons, the Algonkians were a nomadic race, constantly on the move. They needed a home that could be built quickly from materials at hand, and the wigwam was the answer.

Dome-shaped, it is built by cutting stout saplings, and placing the butt ends firmly in the ground forming a circle. These are then bent over to form a dome and lashed together. A door opening is left and the frame is then covered with sheets of bark or hides. These dwellings could be put up in a very short time. When a move took place, only the bark covering was taken along; fresh poles were cut at the new site.

In this area of the compound are tall fuel piles of drying wood, typical Huron smokehouses used to dry fish and meat, a few crude lean-to's which provided quick shelter, and fire-rings here and there in the grass.

Indians not yet baptized st
this outer compound. N
well in the foreground,
log steps leading to ar
lookout p

Father Lalement in 1644 wrote of "a sort of a hospital outside our apartments". This is in the Christian Indian compound. The sick and injured were in the capable hands of Le Sieur François Gendron who trained at Hôtel-Dieu d'Orléan, and arrived at Sainte-Marie in 1643. He returned to France and became doctor to the royal family and later was honoured by the king for his work.

Indian Hospital

The hospital building is forty-feet by forty-four feet, built as the other European structures, with two rows of two-inch horizontal planks packed with clay and stone for insulation. The building is divided by a partitioning wall which does not have a doorway. A statement in the Jesuit *Relations* reads, "the hospital is so distinct from our dwelling that not only men and children, but even women can be admitted to it." This indicates that one room of the hospital was set aside for female Indian patients.

In the west wall of the building is a large fireplace with a built-in warming oven which provided warmth as well as a means of heating up food brought from the cookhouse. On one side there are work tables and shelves which hold wooden vessels, mortars and other

The hospital in the Christian Indian compound. Notice the domed Algonkian wigwam in the background.

utensils. A beautiful table stands near the fireplace. Several beds range along each wall in both rooms, and the few windows are covered with scraped skins.

A projection wing, sixteen feet by ten feet, extends from the northwest corner where the apothecary, Joseph Molère, was located. This small dispensary is shelf-lined with a mixing table nearby. While it is not known what drugs and herbs were used, in Quebec aloes, senna, squill, scammony, calomel and almond oil were in common use, and it is likely that some, if not all, of these reached Sainte-Marie. Herbs which the Indians used were likely to be in the dispensary. Raisins and lemon peel were at hand, but drugs were very scarce, and a popular cure for sickness was bleeding.

Sainte-Marie was a busy place. In April 1648, Father Ragueneau writes:

81

This house is a resort for the whole country, where Christians find a hospital in their sickness, a refuge in the height of alarms, and a hospice when they come to visit us. During the past year we have reckoned over 3,000 persons to whom we have given shelter . . . sometimes within a fortnight six or seven hundred Christians, and as a rule three meals to each one. This does not include a large number who incessantly come hither to pass the whole day, and to whom we also give charity; so that, in a strange country, we feed those who themselves should supply us with the necessities of life.

Beds in the hospital have cedar branches as mattresses.

A corner of the pharmacy.

Indian Mission Church

The spiritual life of Sainte-Marie grew by leaps and bounds from the early 1640's onward. In 1642 the Jesuits constructed a church for the Indians in the north-west corner of their own compound. The Indian Mission Church of Saint-Joseph is built like the structures in the European compound. There is no flooring, just hard-packed, white sand, and there is a large fireplace at each end. On the simple altar are vestments, altar cloths, altar cards and candles. Two unusual candelabra stand at either side. There are no pews in the church, leaving it open and clear as in the Jesuit Chapel. Adjacent to the church is a cemetery. There is evidence that the church was also used as a school.

Today there is a Pilgrim's Walk along the west palisade, which passes through a gate in the palisade and a door in the west wall. The Walk leads to Jean de Brébeuf's grave, marked by a flat stone slab and surrounded by a palisade of iron poles. Here the faithful can pay homage to a martyr of their church.

Father Brébeuf, however, was not the only person to be buried within the walls of Sainte-Marie, for in the cemetery next to the Indian Church lie the graves of twenty Indians and one European. All indications are that the remains of the white man are those of Jacques Douart who came to Sainte-Marie as a boy in 1642, and in 1646 at the age of twenty took the vows of a *donné*. On April 28, 1648, Douart "wandered a short distance from the house . . . and was

The Indian chapel,
Canada's first religious shrine,
the first permanent church in Ontario.

killed by a blow from a hatchet." He was the victim of a plot instigated by non-Christian Indians. Two brothers were employed and they had "started that very day from a distance of five leagues, with the design of killing the first Frenchman whom they might meet alone."

A council was held in which the Hurons were divided among themselves. The Christians remained loyal to the Jesuits, the non-believers desired to do away with the Jesuits and French whom they blamed for the evils that were befalling them. Nor did the Jesuits treat the matter lightly for all Indians had been barred from Sainte-Marie. It was finally settled according to Huron custom and reparations in the form of presents were made to the French by the whole Huron nation. By this time the Hurons realized they could not afford to lose the friendship and assistance of the French.

The altar of the Indian church.

...orner of the Indian church. Note the rolled deerskin window covering and primitive candelabra.

At the southernmost tip of Sainte-Marie is the area designated for the non-baptized. It generally parallels the outside walls, narrowing in places to only a few yards wide. The framework of a second long-house, a few lean-to's and fuel piles dot the compound, and a well with a long sweep-pole provides fresh water for the visitor.

Following the natural formation of the land, the outside walls meet on a slight knoll at the apex of a triangle. Here is a five-sided, cedar-log bastion, built in a similar manner to pioneer log buildings. Each wall is sixteen feet long with a projection of one foot at each corner. Because of the natural cover furnished to raiding canoes by the bullrushes, a constant watch was necessary. It was provided by this high, timber stronghold with loopholes in the second storey. From this triangular tip a watch could be kept over an extensive area of the Wye River and the hills around the lake.

In every way Sainte-Marie was built to endure. Its walls were of stone sunk deep into the earth. Its buildings were laid on firm foundations. Its plan was an amazing pattern of traditional European architecture adapted to a remote wilderness location, and to the purpose of ministering to a stone-age people.

Sainte-Marie's cemetery near the Indian chapel. The grave of Douart, a Frenchman who met death at the hands of the Hurons, is marked with a flat wooden marker and carved cross.

Inside a Huron longhouse.

PART FOUR

THE CURTAIN FALLS

Even as Sainte-Marie grew and prospered, all was far from well beyond the fort and along its lifeline to Quebec, for the hostility of the Iroquois was mounting in fury. No longer was ancient tribal war little more than an exercise for Huron and Iroquois braves; it had grown into a bitter conflict—with the rich fur trade as the spoils of the winter.

Long before, when Champlain had first come to Canada, he had realized that the French must make a choice between supporting either Huron or Iroquois. He knew that the Hurons controlled the rich northern fur trade which was flowing down the St. Lawrence to Quebec; he knew, too, that what furs the Iroquois might secure would go down the Hudson River to the rival Dutch West Indian Company. His choice was obvious: in 1609 he led a Huron war party against the Iroquois. From that moment forward, the Iroquois became deadly enemies of the French and their Huron allies. Again in 1615 he joined a Huron war party against the Iroquois, which aggravated the breach.

Now committed to the Hurons, the French and the Hurons pursued their fur trade, suffering little more than sporadic Iroquois raids against Huron flotillas on their way to Quebec, and against French outposts. But as the early years of the seventeenth century passed, and the Iroquois grew in strength, a system of defense had to be set up along the fur trade route to protect both the trade and missionary undertakings in far-off Huronia. A fort at Trois Rivières was erected in 1634, and a palisaded stronghold at Montreal in 1643.

The vast stretch of the Ottawa River was left unprotected; the French gave little help to the Hurons in the way of muskets and ammunition, or with armed escorts on the dangerous journey to and from Huronia.

The years went on until the early 1640's. In the meantime the Iroquois, still smarting under the manner in which the French had aided their enemies, were laying a formidable plan to annihilate the hated Hurons. The Iroquois were now nearing the height of their powers. Their war chieftains sat long in conclave, not planning the small and insignificant summer raids on Huronia as in the past, but setting out an overall strategy to destroy Huronia, once and for all. The spur that brought them to this was the fact that they were running short of furs, while the Hurons had an abundant supply. There was only one way for the Iroquois to get those furs, and that was to destroy the Hurons.

Encouraged, and perhaps guided to some extent by the Dutch fur traders of the Hudson River, the Iroquois prepared their offensive. The Dutch, avid for those rich furs that were now flowing to the French in Quebec, supplied the Iroquois with muskets and ammunition, and spurred them on.

The Iroquois campaign against the Hurons began even while the first buildings of Sainte-Marie were rising. Fur brigades from Huronia returned to report heavy casualties; Iroquois ambushes on the Ottawa River were no longer occasional; at almost every night camp, an attack and a fight occurred.

Huron chieftains solemnly discussed the situation amidst the flickering fires of the community longhouse. If they sent their braves down the Ottawa and the St. Lawrence on escort duty with the fur canoes, then their home villages would be open to attack. On the other hand, if their warriors stayed home to protect their villages, they would soon run out of the French supplies upon which they had come to depend.

By now, the fur trade was vital to them. No longer were they content to live as they had done before the white man came. European tools of iron, the copper cooking pots, the needles, awls, knives and axes and many other things were essential to their life.

In 1642, barely three years after the founding of Sainte-Marie, the hazards of the fur brigades from Huronia to Quebec were described in a letter of Father Vimont, Superior of Quebec, who wrote:

There are two divisions of Iroquois. . . . The settlement of the Dutch is near them; they go thither to carry on their trades, especially in arquebuses; they have at present three hundred of these, and use them with skill and boldness. These are the ones who make incursions upon our Algonkians and Montagnais, and watch the Hurons at all places along the River, slaughtering them, burning them, and carrying off their Peltry, which they sell to the Dutch, in order to have powder and arquebuses, and then to ravage everything and become masters everywhere, which is fairly easy for them unless France gives us help. For, sundry contagious diseases having consumed the greater part of the Montagnais and the Algonkians, who are neighbours to us, they have nothing to fear on their side; and, moreover, the Hurons who come down, coming for trade and not for war, and having not arquebus, if they are met, have no other defense but flight; and if they are captured, they allow themselves to be bound and massacred like sheep.

In former years, the Iroquois came in rather large bands at certain times in the Summer, and afterwards left the River free, but this present year, they have changed their plan, and have separated themselves into small bands of twenty, thirty, fifty or a hundred at the most, along all the passages and places of the River, and when one band goes away, another succeeds it. They are merely small troops well armed, which set out incessantly, one after the other, from the country of the Iroquois, in order to occupy the whole great River, and to lay ambushes along it everywhere; from these they issue unexpectedly, and fall indifferently upon the Montagnais, Algonkians, Hurons and French.

During the 1640's the Huron fur brigades persisted, fighting off Iroquois attacks as best they could. It was on the Ottawa River that they suffered most, where well-armed bands of Iroquois lay in ambush to hit them at every opportunity.

And then in 1642, the long-range plan of the Iroquois to annihilate Huronia moved into its second stage. Meeting no determined resistance to their raids on the fur brigades, they now went at Huronia in earnest. In the early summer they struck a massive blow, hitting the outlying Huron village of Contarrea, a few miles south-west of the present town of Orillia. Every man, woman and child within its walls was killed, and the village put to the torch. There were no Jesuits in the settlement for they had been refused permission even to talk to its inhabitants.

Wild alarm spread among other Huron towns which expected an immediate Iroquois attack—but it did not come. The Iroquois had satisfied themselves that the Hurons, peaceful and less skilled in planned tribal battles, could wait until the more militant tribes of the St. Lawrence and Ottawa River areas were subdued.

After the destruction of Contarrea, the Iroquois began a ruthless campaign to subdue the friends and allies of the Hurons. In the years that followed, they methodically attacked the tribes fringing the Hurons. Petuns, Neutrals and Algonkian refugees filtered into Huron country. Huronia was slowly being isolated for the final kill.

The Jesuits urged the authorities in France to send military aid to Huronia, but France paid little attention to such pleas. A few soldiers were sent to Sainte-Marie, but there was no concerted effort made to protect Huronia from the impending invasion. In the meantime, Sainte-Marie prospered. In 1645, Jérôme Lalemant passed over his post of Superior to Paul Ragueneau. Saint-Marie had by now become a mecca of faith in the Huron country, a centre where people sought help, advice and protection.

Facing the wild marshes to the south, the five-sided bastion looks out over an area once feared by the inhabitants of Sainte-Marie. From the loopholes just under the eaves a watch was kept for possible Iroquois attackers.

The years went on, and by 1648 a dozen or more outlying mission stations dotted Huronia and the country beyond. Among these were old Saint-Joseph II, which Brébeuf had established, Saint-Ignace II, about seven miles away and others such as Saint-Louis, Saint-John and Saint-Michel.

Disquieting news of more and more frequent Iroquois raids, and rumours of Iroquois plans to attack Huronia, led to the abandonment of such far-flung missions as Saint-Jean Baptiste on Lake Simcoe. By 1648, old Saint-Joseph II, the ancient village of Teanaostaiae, was the outermost palisaded town in Huronia. Here Father Antoine Daniel had laboured for four years with marked success. His converts were many, and he was revered and loved by Indians far and wide.

It was here that the Iroquois first struck in force.

On the morning of July 4, 1648, the town was quiet and peaceful. Most of its warriors were absent, either trading, or hunting or on hostile expeditions. Father Daniel had just finished conducting Mass in his chapel when the dreaded cry "The Iroquois! The Iroquois!" rang out over the town. Father Ragueneau reports:

He had hardly finished the usual mass after sunrise and the Christians, who had assembled in considerable numbers, had not yet left the sacred house, when, at the war-cry of the enemy, in haste and alarm they seized their weapons. Some rush into the fight and others flee headlong; everywhere is terror, everywhere lamentation.

Antoine hastened wherever he saw the danger most threatening, inspiring not only the Christians with Christian strength, but many unbelievers with faith.

That he may delay the enemy, and, like a good shepherd, aid the escape of his flock, he blocks the way of the armed men and breaks their onset; a simple man against the foe. At last he fell, mortally wounded by a musket shot and pierced with arrows. Savagely enraged against his lifeless body, hardly one of the enemy was there who did not add a new wound to his corpse, until at length, the church having been set on fire, his naked body was cast into the flames and was so completely consumed that not even a bone was left.

The village was soon a heap of glowing ashes. Hundreds of Hurons had been killed, and nearly 700 prisoners cringed under Iroquois guards. A nearby small village was burned. The Iroquois stole away after having dealt Huronia the worst blow it had ever received. Over 2,000 people had lived in Teanaostaiaé, and only a handful escaped into the forest.

Huronia was paralyzed with fear for its people knew now that the full force of the Iroquois was being loosed against them at last. Scouts brought the news that over 1,200 of their enemies were wintering on the upper Ottawa, awaiting the spring to renew attacks.

Although the Jesuit Fathers implored the Hurons to strengthen their defences and prepare for the coming invasion, they did nothing. They were like a doomed people, sunk in dejection, fearing everything. Their warriors lay idle in the towns, refusing to believe that the Iroquois would dare penetrate the heart of their land. Nothing could arouse them to face the imminent danger.

The fall of 1648 went into winter with the Hurons hopefully believing that the Iroquois might go away. But in March of 1649 the invaders struck again and the ruin of Huronia began.

Saint-Ignace II, about seven miles from Sainte-Marie, was now a frontier village. It was strongly fortified and was the site of a mission under the care of the veteran, Brébeuf, and Gabriel Lalemant, a nephew of Jérôme Lalemant. Between Saint-Ignace II and Saint-Marie lay Saint-Louis, about three miles away.

Before daylight on March 16, the Iroquois burst through the palisades at the weakest point, fell upon the sleeping Hurons and killed many with knives and hatchets, and took a large number as prisoners. Two or three Hurons escaped and fled to Saint-Louis, with hundreds of war-crazed Iroquois close behind. Brébeuf and Lalemant had spent the night at Saint-Louis. Begging the two priests to fly to Sainte-Marie, the eighty warriors in Saint-Louis decided to fight. Brébeuf and Lalemant stayed with them. In minutes, the Iroquois were at the palisades, hacking and burning to force an entrance. The outcome was inevitable. Though the Hurons fought bravely the town was soon overwhelmed and all the survivors made prisoner, including the two priests.

The town was fired and the prisoners were marched back to Saint-Ignace where Brébeuf and Lalement were cruelly tortured and finally killed. Now the Iroquois divided into smaller bands to burn neighbouring villages and hunt the fleeing inhabitants. In the afternoon, scouts reconnoitred Saint-Marie itself with the idea of attacking it the next day.

While Huron fugitives poured into Sainte-Marie, Father Ragueneau, with forty well-armed Frenchmen, prepared for the attack which they felt must surely come. But it did not materialize, for on the morning of March 17, 300 Huron warriors arrived at Sainte-Marie just in time to intercept an advance part of about 200 Iroquois on their way to open an attack on the mission. The invaders were driven back to the shattered palisades of Saint-Louis, then routed towards Saint-Ignace where the main body of Iroquois lay waiting.

Wild with rage, the Iroquois surged back towards Saint-Louis. Then took place one of the fiercest Indian battles on record. Only 150 Huron warriors crouched behind the battered palisades of Saint-Louis. The Iroquois, over 1,000 strong, were well armed with guns, of which the Hurons had few.

94

This Pilgrim's Walk on the we
side of Sainte-Marie leads to t
Grave of Brébeuf in the Indi
church which is always ke
open to the pub

The Hurons fought with mad and reckless ferocity, driving back their assailants again and again. All day long the battle raged. No quarter was given or asked. Bodies piled high amidst the ruined walls. Under the cover of darkness, the Iroquois finally burst into the Huron ranks to find only twenty men alive. They were killed to the last man.

But Sainte-Marie had been saved for the time being. The Iroquois had had enough of such fighting. They herded most of their Huron captives—old men, women and children—into the huts of Saint-Ignace, bound them to stakes and set fire to the village. No one escaped the holocaust. The next day, with the rest of their prisoners and laden with plunder and baggage, the Iroquois set out southward.

Behind them most of Huronia lay in ruins. Smoke from smouldering Huron villages drifted in palls over the land. The terrified Hurons had scattered like frightened sheep. Many stumbled into Sainte-Marie, others fled through the spring snows to the Petun country, still

others made their way to Algonkian villages to the north and to the Neutrals far to the south.

Panic swept everything before it. Huron joined Petun to flee the country. It is recorded that a number of these refugees wandered as far as the Oklahoma area of the United States. Still other Hurons sought adoption among their victorious enemies.

Huronia was virtually conquered. Its villages, its chapels, its fields and its life had been destroyed. Without a leader, without organization the Hurons simply fled:

These poor, distressed people, forsook their lands, houses and villages, in order to escape the cruelty of an enemy whom they feared more than a thousand deaths. Many, no longer expecting humanity from man, flung themselves into the deepest recesses of the forest, where, though it were with wild beasts, they might find peace. (Ragueneau)

The Jesuit Fathers set out to follow and console the scattered bands, but little could be done. Within two weeks of the destruction of Saint-Louis and Saint-Ignace, fifteen Huron towns had been abandoned and many burned so that they would not provide the enemy with shelter.

During the Jesuits' last days at Sainte-Marie, it must have looked much like this from the far side of the Wye River.

Sadly, Father Ragueneau faced a grim fact, best described in his letter to Rome:

There are here eighteen Fathers. . . . Truly, we are so threatened by the hostile rage of our savage enemies that, unless we wish our enterprise and ourselves to perish in an hour, it was quite necessary for us to seek the protection of these men, who devote themselves to both domestic and farm work. . . . For until late years our abode . . . was surrounded on every side by the numerous villages of our friends, the Hurons, we feared more for them than ourselves from hostile attack; so during that time, however small our number, we lived in safety, without anxiety. But now, far different is the aspect of our affairs and of this whole region; for so crushed are our Hurons by disasters, that, their outposts being taken and laid waste with fire and sword, most of them have been forced to change their abodes, and retreat elsewhere; hence it has come to pass that at last we are devoid of the protection of others, and now we, stationed at the front, must defend ourselves with our own strength, our own courage and our own members.

Sainte-Marie stood alone. Its mission was over. The Hurons had fled and with them the reason for Sainte-Marie's existence was gone. To remain would be inviting destruction, for the Iroquois would surely be back, and Sainte-Marie would bear the brunt of the next attack. It would be rash and useless to attempt to save the mission. Sainte-Marie would have to be abandoned!

Out of the chaos of the spring of 1649, emerged a few Huron leaders who implored the Fathers to help the Huron nation reunite. They met at Sainte-Marie and chose to live on Manitoulin Island, where they would have access to Algonkian tribes and would be nearer to the French settlements. Fishing was good and so was the soil. Then twelve Huron chiefs arrived to say that many of the scattered Hurons were determined to reunite and form a settlement on Isle St. Joseph, or Christian Island. In a conference with the Fathers they persuaded the Jesuits to join the Hurons on Christian Island, about twenty miles away and some three miles off the shore in Georgian Bay. While Huron scouts searched the bush for survivors, Father Ragueneau and his men made ready to move.

In early May the task of evacuating Sainte-Marie began. A large boat and several log rafts were constructed. Sainte-Marie was stripped of everything that could be moved: first the stock of corn, then weapons, ammunition, tools, goods for barter, pictures, vestments, sacred vessels and images, and finally the cattle, swine and poultry. On the afternoon of June 14, all was ready. The laden boat and rafts lay on the quiet river before Sainte-Marie.

It would have been folly to leave the strongly fortified Sainte-Marie to become an Iroquois fort. It had been built to endure; its walls were sunk deep into the earth, its buildings lay on firm foundations:

But on each of us lay the necessity of bidding farewell to that old home of Sainte-Marie, to its structures, which though plain, seemed in the eyes of our poor savages, master-works of art; and to its cultivated lands, which were promising us an abundant harvest. It was necessary to abandon . . . our home . . . for fear that the enemies would profane this holy place in taking shelter. We set fire to it ourselves and we saw burning in front of our eyes, in less than an hour, our work of nine or ten years.

The journey to Christian Island was made safely. Here the priests found some 300 Huron families living in the woods. Father Ragueneau's party which included forty soldiers, labourers and other, set to work at once. Before winter came the new mission, called Sainte-Marie II, was completed. It was built as a fort according to military standards. There were thick stone walls, fourteen feet high, with stone bastions at each corner. Inside it had a chapel, houses for lodging and a well. Surrounding the entire stronghold was a moat making it quite impregnable.

By the fall of 1649, almost every Huron survivor had gathered on Christian Island under the protection of the French fort. There were 8,000 of them, and now began a year of horror. While the Fathers made every effort to secure smoked fish and acorns from the Algonkians to the north, it was impossible to find food for all. Hundreds died of starvation even before the cruel winter set in. Bands of Iroquois patrolled the mainland, so that to venture into the woods for game meant certain death. Father Ragueneau, his French companions, and the thousands of Hurons were virtual prisoners on Christian Island.

December came, and with it news that Iroquois war parties were headed for the remaining missions in Petun country. Father Ragueneau at once sent runners to Fathers Garnier and Chabanel to warn them of the danger, but it was too late. Garnier was caught and murdered in an attack on Saint-Jean; Chabanel was killed while making his way to Sainte-Marie II. Now the Iroquois began to lay waste the Petun country. Only one small mission remained in mainland Huronia, at an isolated spot in the Blue Hills where Fathers Greslon and Garreau still carried on.

The harsh winter of 1649-50 brought great suffering to Christian Island. While the Iroquois prowled the mainland three miles away, ready to pounce on anyone who ventured there in search of game, The Hurons on Christian Island starved. Acorns, treebark, all the dogs, even skin clothing went into the cooking pots. Then cannibalism followed, despite all efforts to stop it. There is no more horrible record of suffering in the pages of Canadian history than that of the Hurons on Christian Island during that terrible winter. By Spring 1650, well over 4,000 of them had died, and the rest were walking skeltons.

When the warm weather came, those still able to move about stole to the mainland, only to meet death at the hands of the Iroquois. "My pen," writes Father Ragueneau, "has no ink black enough to describe the fury of the Iroquois." By June 1650, about 300 Hurons were left alive. Father Ragueneau knew by now that it was impossible to stay in Huronia any longer. The Fathers from the isolated mission in the Blue Hills had safely returned to Sainte-Marie II. Huronia was empty.

Huron chieftains consulted with the Jesuits who resolved to try to save the remnants of the nation by leading them to Quebec where there was some hope of safety. Father Ragueneau and 360 French and Hurons abandoned the fort on June 10, 1650. They arrived safely in Quebec on July 28.

Of the twenty-five Fathers who had toiled in Huronia, five had met a martyr's death. Isaac Jogues, the man who had built the first house in Sainte-Marie had died in the land of the Iroquois in what is now northern New York State. Two other Jesuits also died there.

The Huron mission was at an end.

PART FIVE

AFTERWARDS

For a hundred years Huronia lay empty except for wandering tribes of Ojibwas who kept open some of the old Huron trails. The wilderness closed in around Sainte-Marie I and Sainte-Marie II. The living forest crept over the ruins, gradually concealing the scars of destruction.

Sainte-Marie and its site were almost forgotten, but its sturdy masonry, pushing up amidst the grass, weeds and trees became a landmark as early as 1789, when William Claus, on behalf of the Crown, signed a land treaty with the Ojibwas and described the lands as: "Beginning at the head or south-westernmost angle of a bay situated *above certain French ruins* now lying on the east side of a small strait leading from the said Bay . . . ." In 1793, when John Graves Simcoe visited the Georgian Bay country, a member of his party made a map of the journey on which is shown "French ruins supposed to be the Church of St. Mary's".

In 1815, the Government of Upper Canada took over the southern part of the present county of Simcoe by treaty with the Indians. A somewhat haphazard survey followed and the land was put up for grant. The historic site of Sainte-Marie became simply a portion of Lot 16, Concession 3 in the newly formed township of Tay. In 1819 it was granted to one Samuel Richardson, a Welsh land surveyor. He failed to meet the terms of the grant, and in 1830 the site became the property of Pierre Rondeau, a fur trader and veteran of the War of 1812.

These men were the first to legally own the historic acres of Sainte-Marie. The stones of its ancient walls still showed above the ground. They were pried apart to build the foundations and fireplaces of settlers' cabins. The old French ruins on the banks of the River Wye meant nothing to the newcomers.

In the years that followed the site of Sainte-Marie roused the interest of many people. In 1844 Jesuit Father Pierre Chazelle visited the site and then wrote to France, urging that the ruins be excavated. Six years later, in 1850, Father Joseph Hanipaux did the same. In 1852, the Rev. George Hallen, first rector of the Garrison Church of St. James-on-the-Lines at Penetanguishene, spent considerable time at the ruins, and drew maps and charts which have since proved invaluable. In 1855, Jesuit Father Félix Martin spent two weeks in Huronia and added considerably to the growing knowledge of its extent. Twenty years later, Peter Brunet, a public land surveyor drew a map of the old mission fort, and in 1878 Professor John Galbraith of the University of Toronto visited the site and also drew a map of Sainte-Marie. James Bain of the Toronto Library presented a paper to the Canadian Institute in April, 1885, covering the "present condition of the old fort of Sainte-Marie", in which he pointed out that souvenir hunters and local residents were steadily razing the ruins. In 1890 David Byle described the ruins and urged that something be done to stop further damage.

By now, scholars and historians were well aware of the historical significance of Sainte-Marie. In 1891 members of the Canadian Institute unsuccessfully attempted to purchase the site by public subscription; then interest in the project subsided.

In 1899, Andrew F. Hunter made quite an extensive report on the condition of the ruins, and in 1909 the Bureau of Archives produced a monumental work by Jesuit Father Arthur Edward Jones on Huronia and Sainte-Marie.

Nothing of any importance was done to reconstruct or preserve Sainte-Marie until 1940, when the site was purchased by the Society of Jesus of the Province of Upper Canada. The acres of the ancient mission fort were at last removed from private ownership and what stones remained were safe from further pilfering.

People were becoming aware of the real significance of Sainte-Marie, although its ancient glory still lay hidden under the scrub of weeds and beneath the tough roots of century-old elms. Excavations

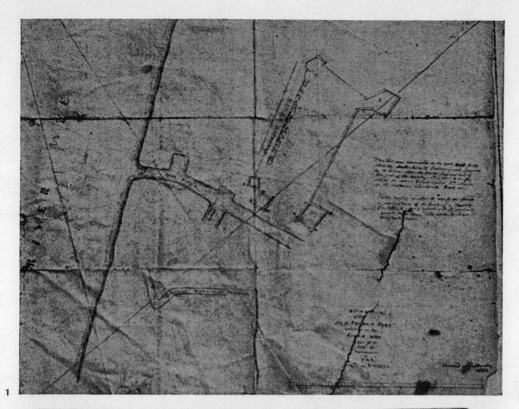

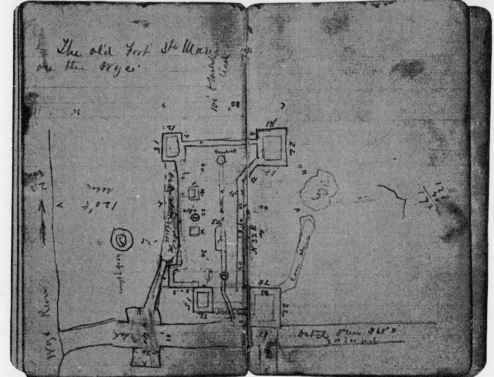

Two early maps of the site:
1. Drawn by the Rev. George Hallen (1852).
2. Drawn by Prof. John Galbraith (1878).

were started in 1941 and continued until 1943. The project was carried out by the Royal Ontario Museum, University of Toronto, under the direction of Mr. Kenneth E. Kidd, whose explorations were confined to the area outlined by stone remains.

But in 1947, other evidence came to light which led to the conviction that Sainte-Marie was far larger than the outline of the stonework. Workmen found a charred line of blackened timber mould leading beyond the territory considered to be the boundary of Sainte-Marie. There was also a queer moat which had never been fully explained.

In June 1948, Dr. Wilfrid Jury, then curator of the Museum of Indian Archaeology of the University of Western Ontario, set about to sift the truth from the soil. He dug, and dug and dug. He and his young crews literally dissolved the soil. For four long, painstaking years, from 1948 to 1951, the earth was gently removed, layer by layer, piece by piece. Using everything from shovel and axe to delicate camel hair brushes, he and his companions uncovered evidence which has made possible the accurate reconstruction of Sainte-Marie.

They found positive proof of an amazing European settlement. The earth was their mentor, for earth alone has a queer quality of remembrance. Sink a pole or a timber into the earth today and centuries later it will retain a patterned stain in the soil around it.

Scene during the early months of reconstruction of the European Compound.

As Jury and his crews shaved the earth of Sainte-Marie, a majestic plan came to light. Post moulds outlined buildings. When the ground was dug within these outlines, ancient cellars yielded evidence of the use of the building once above and lines of brown stains in a soil of amber marked ancient outlying palisades. Under chemical analysis, the soil gave clues to what had existed on the surface 300 years ago.

Dr. Jury's work revealed a story so filled with interest and deep historical significance that knowledge of it alone did not seem enough. Through his painstaking work, the plan and features of Sainte-Marie lay plain. Sainte-Marie could live again if funds and facilities were provided for its restoration. But because of the enormous cost the project was beyond the resources of any single group.

Old stonework is unearthed during excavation by Dr. Jury (centre) and colleagues.

Excavated remains of a root cellar.

⹁n axehead found during the excavation of the blacksmith shop.

On March 19, 1964, the Prime Minister of Ontario, the Hon. John F. Robarts, announced the formation of the Huronia Historical Development Council for the prime purpose of reconstructing Sainte-Marie-among-the-Hurons. This five-man Committee includes representatives of the Ontario Government, the University of Western Ontario, and the Society of Jesus. The university accepted responsibility for the reconstruction work, and for the necessary research to ensure authenticity.

With Dr. Jury in charge, work was started on June 15, 1964. Intensive research began as all written records were thoroughly searched. Although the earth had yielded all its evidence, there was not a scrap of information to indicate how Sainte-Marie appeared above the ground, nor were there any records or documents which provided it. In the Jesuit *Relations*, annual reports sent back to the French headquarters, there were several references to Sainte-Marie, and to the presence of various structures, but absolutely no detail about those structures. Bit by bit, casual remarks written about the buildings were assembled from dozens of sources. For example,

In reconstructing Sainte-Marie, building practices of early times were employed. Here the log walls of the stable are being chinked with moss and clay.

Stonemasons
followed Norman
techniques in
reconstructing
the walls.

Squaring timber for the
reconstruction.

there was mentioned in the writings of a Jesuit stationed at Sainte-Marie an incident which occurred when a blind Indian woman approached one of the four tall crosses which stood at each corner of the mission. Seeking to touch the cross, she was hindered by pickets, but reached through with a stick to touch the holy symbol. From this brief reference, it was concluded that each of the four crosses was enclosed by pickets.

Depositories in Canada, the United States, France, Belgium, Italy, Austria and the Soviet Union were searched. Because most of the men of Sainte-Marie had originally come from Normandy, particularly the artisans and builders, it is reasonably certain that Sainte-Marie's buildings would have been typical of seventeenth century Norman architecture. To become acquainted with the structures of this period, methods of construction, crafts, trades and furnishings, Dr. Jury and his associates spent some time in the Province of Quebec, and in Normandy, France, where grizzled artisans told of ways of building which have not changed in hundreds of years.

Dr. Jury (right) and an assistant excavate the waterway at its entrance to the Wye River.

Evidence of the waterway comes to light during excavations.

111

Dormers were a feature of seventeenth century Norman architecture. Note the window latch made from a peg and a small piece of leather.

A hammered iron door latch, typical of the handcrafted iron work to be seen frequently at Sainte-Marie

A window of scraped deerskin. Hides were carefully scraped until they were quite thin, thus permitting some light to pass through.

The bellows of ancient forges, the hand-wrought hinges of old doors, seventeenth century lamps still existed. The ingenious methods of Norman furniture-makers and almost all the skills of the seventeenth century artisans were still sharp in the minds of many rural craftsmen, and from them came details to supplement the discoveries on Sainte-Marie's site.

Slowly the puzzle was joined, piece by piece. Details of the very first buildings in New France were studied, the oldest buildings in Quebec City were closely examined. From the Palais de Justice at Quebec and Montreal, the ancient contracts of carpenters, masons and builders were scanned, and from these came invaluable information on Canada's first houses, granaries and churches.

From the precious records of the Jesuit Order, from museums far and wide, from eminent historians and scholars, from contemporary writings of the period, a vivid picture of Sainte-Marie gradually took shape.

Reconstruction of Sainte-Marie's stonework followed masonry methods of the time.

Armed with every scrap of information available, and with the evidence he had found in the soil, Dr. Jury set to work. Plans of every building were drawn. Jury himself built detailed models of every structure, and the actual work began.

Local French-Canadian craftsmen did the job utilizing fifteenth century skills of hand-chopping, broad-axing, adzing and working with stone. At many points in Sainte-Marie today, the original stone may be seen, just as it was first placed in position in the 1640's.

To visit Sainte-Marie today is to step back in time more than 300 years and live momentarily in this amazing wilderness mission which flourished in Canada's earliest years. The idea behind restoring Sainte-Marie was not to display a series of exhibits, but to create an environment of living history. We may see and touch and handle the corn pestles in the cookhouse, the furs on the platforms of the Huron longhouse. We may rest for a moment on a bench identical with those which once were used by Sainte-Marie's own people. We may heft a sledge once used by the builders of this stronghold. As we walk around the grounds and buildings, the warm smell of wood smoke is everywhere, for fires are kept smouldering in the

Sainte-Marie takes shape in early years of reconstruction.

Dr. Jury and the foreman in a south court dwelling.

restored fireplaces. In the cookhouse the odour of drying herbs, corn, sunflower and sage hanging from the ceiling adds a tart tinge to the air. At intervals, the soft clamour of an ancient bell high in the peak of the chapel adds a sound of old Sainte-Marie to the scene.

Sainte-Marie is still growing as bits of further evidence turn up to establish more and more of its life. Constant study and research continue. Buildings are being linked with the known inhabitants of the mission, such as the small dwelling which has been marked as the possible quarters of Charles Boivin. Pieces of furniture are being slowly added, for they must be made by hand with ancient tools if they are to carry out the authenticity of Sainte-Marie.

It is unquestionably one of Canada's most historic treasures. Here we may momentarily share in the lives and times of Canada's first European community deep in the wilderness. Here, for a brief span of ten years, a bright spark of civilization glowed and met its end in sacrifice.

115

RESEARCH ON SAINTE-MARIE

In the restoration of Sainte-Marie, a vast amount of research was carried out by Dr. Jury and his associates. Searches were made in Canadian, the United States and in European depositories as follows:

CANADA
The Public Archives of Canada, Ottawa.
The Provincial Archives of Quebec, Quebec City.
The Archives of the Ursuline Convent, Quebec City.
The Archives of the Quebec Seminary, Quebec City.
The Archives of the Hôtel Dieu, Quebec City.
Saint Mary's College, Montreal.
The University of Montreal, Montreal.
McGill University, Montreal.
The Archives of the Palais de Justice, at Montreal,
Quebec City and Three Rivers, Quebec.
Bibliothèque, St. Sulpice, Montreal.

UNITED STATES
John Carter Brown Library, Brown University,
Providence, Rhode Island.

Riggs Library, Georgetown University,
Washington, D.C.

FRANCE
Work was carried out through the representative of the Canadian Archives with respect to the Archives and Libraries of Paris, departmental libraries of the French Government and archives of the various departments of France. The available papers of Cardinal Richelieu were also searched.

Through the co-operation of the Vicar-General of the Jesuit Order, Canadian documents in the libraries and archives of Jesuit Colleges and Residences in France were thoroughly researched. Such places as the Archives des Seine-Maritime at Rouen, Hôtel Dieu at Dieppe and various museums were visited.

BELGIUM
Jesuit letters and various other materials were checked in Brussels.

ROME
A special search was made on Father Bressani, the one Italian Jesuit who lived at Sainte-Marie. An important undertaking was the reading of letters in the Gallia Series, which were procured from the Jesuit Archives in Rome. These are letters written by the Jesuit missionaires in Canada to the Jesuit General in Rome.

VIENNA
In view of the once extensive influence of the Holy Roman Empire, holdings of the National Archives at Vienna were investigated through the Canadian legation.

U.S.S.R.
During the latter part of the eighteenth century considerable French archival material was taken to Russia. The Jesuits themselves were established there for some years, chiefly at St. Petersburg. The search was carried out through the Canadian Ambassador to Russia.

GENERAL
In order to become well acquainted with architecture of the period, methods of construction, crafts, trades and furnishings, considerable time was spent in the Province of Quebec, and in the Normandy area of France.

BIBLIOGRAPHY

BROWN, G. W. (ed.). *Dictionary of Canadian Biography, Volume I.* University of Toronto, 1965.

COLBY, CHARLES W. *The Founder of New France* (Chronicles of Canada #3). Glasgow Brook, 1915.

COSTAIN, THOMAS B. *The White and the Gold.* Doubleday, 1954.

CRANSTON, J. HERBERT. *Huronia.* Huronia Historic Sites and Tourist Assn., Midland, 1960.

DIONNE, NARCISSE E. *Samuel de Champlain.* University of Toronto, 1963.

HUNT, GEORGE T. *The Wars of the Iroquois.* University of Wisconsin, 1960.

INNIS, HAROLD A. *The Fur Trade in Canada.* University of Toronto, 1956.

JEFFERYS, C. W. *Picture Gallery of Canadian History, Volume I.* Ryerson, 1942.

JENNESS, DIAMOND. *The Indians of Canada.* The Queen's Printer, Ottawa, 1960.

JURY, WILFRID and ELSIE McLEOD. *Sainte-Marie-Among-the-Hurons.* Oxford, 1965.

KIDD, KENNETH E. *The Excavation of Sainte-Marie I.* University of Toronto, 1940.

LEECHMAN, DOUBLAS. *Native Tribes of Canada.* Gage, 1956.

MARQUIS, THOMAS GUTHRIE. *The Jesuit Missions.* University of Toronto, 1964.

MEALING, S. R. *The Jesuit Relations.* McClelland and Stewart, 1963.

PARKMAN, FRANCIS. *The Jesuits in North America.* Little, Brown, 1867.

—————. *Pioneers of France in the New World.* Little, Brown, 1891.

RAGUENEAU, PAUL S. J. *Shadows over Huronia.* Martyr's Shrine, Midland.

SHAW, J. G. *Saints Lived Here.* Martyr's Shrine, Midland.

TALBOT, FRANCIS, S. J. *Saint Among the Hurons.* Doubleday, 1956.

—————. *Saint Among Savages.* Doubleday, 1961.

TOOKER, ELISABETH. *Ethnography of the Huron Indians,* (Bulletin 190). Smithsonian Institute, Washington.

INDEX